TWAYNE'S WORLD AUTHORS SERIES
A Survey of the World's Literature

CANADA

Joseph Jones, University of Texas, Austin

EDITOR

Earle Birney

TWAS 538

EARLE BIRNEY

By PETER AICHINGER

Le College militaire royal de St. Jean

TWAYNE PUBLISHERS
A DIVISION OF G. K. HALL & CO., BOSTON

Published in 1979 by Twayne Publishers,
A Division of G. K. Hall & Co.
All Rights Reserved

Printed on permanent/durable acid-free paper and bound
in the United States of America

First Printing

Frontispiece photograph of
Earle Birney courtesy of
Earle Birney.

819.1
B619za

Library of Congress Cataloging in Publication Data

Aichinger, Peter, 1933–
Earl Birney.

(Twayne's world authors series ; TWAS 538 : Canada)
Bibliography: p. 172–76
Includes index.
1. Birney, Earle, 1904–
—Criticism and interpretation.
PR9199.3.B44Z553   818'.5'209   79-10808
ISBN 0-8057-6380-5

201968

Contents

About the Author

Preface

Acknowledgments

Chronology

1.	Life and Times	13
2.	Satire and the Comic Spirit	53
3.	Love and Death	73
4.	The Mythological Element	86
5.	Nature Poetry	100
6.	Poetic Technique	121
7.	Conclusion: People and Politics	142
	Notes and References	165
	Selected Bibliography	172
	Index	177

About the Author

Peter Aichinger teaches English at le College militaire royal de St-Jean in St-Jean, Quebec. He is a former officer in the Canadian Army and is a graduate of the Royal Military College, the University of Toronto, and Sussex University. He has also published *The American Soldier in Fiction* (1975).

Preface

One summer day about twenty years ago I was undergoing training as an officer cadet in the Canadian Army at a camp in western Canada. Nature had provided us with a temperature approaching one hundred degrees and a landscape consisting for the most part of sand, buffalo grass, cactus, and poison ivy, and the Canadian Army had thoughtfully complemented nature's efforts by having us dress in woolen socks, heavy boots, and thick black cotton coveralls. During one of the five-minute smoke breaks that punctuated the field exercises, I crept into some scrub oak, seeking shade, and to my surprise and joy found a tattered, coverless paperback novel. It was a copy of Earle Birney's *Turvey*. I began reading, and within a few pages had realized that I had stumbled upon a great comic novel; moreover, the circumstances under which I had found it served as an almost preternatural introduction to the elements of fate and irony which characterize much of Birney's work. I still have that tattered paperback; I reread it many times both as an officer cadet and later as a subaltern, and I had many occasions to recall such passages as that in which a professional army sergeant at Camp Borden in 1942 regards a green but imperious young officer "with that curious combination of astonishment, submission, and contempt which practised sergeants used in addressing foolish subalterns." To me, *Turvey* is still the best and funniest novel ever written about the Canadian Army, and it was therefore with great eagerness that I seized the opportunity to write this book.

It has been my intention to deal with Birney's work as a poet and writer of fiction but not, other than incidentally, with his career as a teacher, a scholar, and an editor. His reputation in these domains is safely established in the memories of his colleagues and students, to say nothing of the scholarly journals, but the purpose of this book is to trace his development as a poet.

In order to deal adequately with Birney's poetic development, and to conform to the general pattern of the books in this series, I have discussed his career up to the present day in an opening section and then dealt in subsequent sections in a more detailed manner with some of his poetry and fiction. Thus, the first section of the book is chronological while the following sections are thematic.

One aspect of Birney's work with which I have not dealt, other than here, is the vexing question of the influence which other poets and writers might have had upon him. It is a question to which Birney has reacted angrily and sardonically in the past, and for good reason. An "influence" hunter of even very mediocre talents would be quick to spot in Birney's work what appears to be a host of borrowings, imitations, and adaptations from the works of other writers. For example, Birney's "Bangkok Boy" resembles e.e. cummings not only in its lack of capitalization and in its layout on the page but even in its rhythm, its tender, elegiac mood, it recalls cummings's moving farewell to Jean Le Nègre in *The Enormous Room*. Similarly, the rhythm of Birney's "Francisco Tresguerras" resembles that of Browning's "The Lost Leader" while the tone of the speaker recalls Browning's voice in "A Toccata of Gallupi." One could go even further in considering the subject of Browning's influence in a poem like "Testimony of a Canadian Educational Leader," a poem which, like Browning's "The Bishop Orders his Tomb at St. Praxed's," is a dramatic monolog whose theme is human venality and whose speaker privately reveals an ambiguous attitude toward the relative merits of this life and the next one.

The fact is that Birney was unquestionably influenced by a host of poets living and dead, extending in an unbroken line from King David to Bill Bissett. We are all part of all that we have met, and Birney has met a lot of poets. Moreover, when he actually does feel inspired by another poet he is quick to acknowledge the fact: consider for example "For maister Geffrey," or "Orphiasco" with its "hammage to Ivy Compton-Burnett," or "First Tree for Frost" whose title is a sincere, if punning, compliment to Robert Frost, whom Birney has publicly called the best of all poets to write about trees and small boys. This steady acknowledgment of indebtedness to other men extends even, perhaps especially, to young poets whose work has not been widely recognized outside their own country; in his *rag & bone shop* (1971) Birney offers explicit thanks "to bp nichol, & his generation for turning me on." In this volume I have occasionally drawn parallels between some passages of Birney's work and similar passages in the works of other writers, but without intending to suggest that one poet has influenced the other.

Preface

Another point that it may be well to clarify is Birney's use of the term "northamerican" to include the inhabitants of both Canada and the United States. The word is a useful one since at their worst the residents of both of these countries do in fact share many of the same outlooks, desires, and defects including materialism, a smugness based on technological superiority, a disregard for the natural world, and an ignorance of other cultures. The speaker in "Appeal to a Lady with a Diaper" may have been signaling his anguish to the wife of either an American or a Canadian; in "i accuse us" Birney damns Canadians as being only more sanctimonious and less candid than the Americans about their participation in the Vietnamese war. Hence, I have used the term "northamerican" wherever possible in this book both because of its utility and because it reflects at least one aspect of Birney's perception of our civilization.

Because of Birney's incessant revising of his work it has been necessary to choose some arbitrary standard for citations. As a result, the citations in this book conform to the versions of the poems found in *The Collected Poems of Earle Birney* unless it is clear from the context that this is not the case.

Acknowledgments

My thanks are due primarily to Earle Birney not only for taking the time to read the manuscript and make careful detailed observations upon it, but also for making prompt accurate replies to a series of requests for information, and for providing moral support and encouragement as the book developed. Earle also sent me the photo for the frontispiece.

My thanks are also due to the Chief Librarian at McGill University who gave me free access to all parts of the library, including the Rare Book room, while I was doing the research for this book. I received similar competent assistance from the staff of the Fisher Rare Books library in the University of Toronto.

From *David and Other Poems, Now is Time, The Strait of Anian, Trial of a City and Other Verse, Ice Cod Bell or Stone, Near False Creek Mouth, Selected Poems: 1940–1960, rag & bone shop, what's so big about GREEN?, Collected Poems,* all by Earle Birney, reprinted by permission of The Canadian Publishers, McClelland and Stewart Limited, Toronto.

Chronology

1904   Born May 13 in Calgary, Alberta (at that time still part of the North West Territories).

1904–   Moved about to various parts of Alberta and British Colum-
1922   bia with his family.

1922   Entered University of British Columbia as a student in engineering.

1926   Graduated with first class honors in English language and Literature.

1926–   Leonard Graduate Fellow at the University of Toronto,
1927   studying Old and Middle English and specializing in Chaucer.

1927–   Teaching Fellow at University of California, Berkeley.
1930

1930–   Instructor at University of Utah.
1932

1932–   Teaching Fellow at University of Toronto.
1933

1933–   Instructor at University of Utah; married Sylvia Johnstone
1934   but separated from her almost immediately.

1934–   Royal Society of Canada Fellow at University of London;
1935   met Esther Bull who returned to Canada with him and married him just before the outbreak of World War II.

1936   Ph.D., University of Toronto; received full-time appointment as lecturer in English at University College, Toronto; marriage to Sylvia Johnstone annulled.

1936–   Literary editor of *Canadian Forum.*
1939

1942   Published *David and Other Poems;* Governor General's Award for Poetry.

1942–   Served as a Selection of Personnel Officer with the Cana-
1945   dian Army in Canada, the United Kingdom and North West Europe; attained rank of major; invalided home; published *Now Is Time;* second Governor General's Award for Poetry.

1945–   Supervisor of Foreign Language Broadcasts to Europe for

1946   the International Service of the Canadian Broadcasting Corporation in Montreal.

1946   Returned to the University of British Columbia as Professor of English; accepted editorship of *Canadian Poetry Magazine* published by the Canadian Authors Association.

1948   *Strait of Anian.*

1949   *Turvey.*

1950   Received the Leacock Medal for humor (for *Turvey*).

1952   *Trial of a City and Other Verse.*

1953   Edited *Twentieth Century Canadian Poetry* (anthology); departed Canada for France on a Canadian Government Overseas Fellowship to work on *Down the Long Table;* elected to Royal Society of Canada.

1955   *Down the Long Table*

1958-   Nuffield Foundation Resident Fellow in the British Museum
1959   doing research on Chaucer.

1962   *Ice Cod Bell or Stone;* edited *Selected Poems of Malcolm Lowry.*

1962-   Reading tour in the Caribbean and South America on a
1963   Canada Council Grant.

1964   *Near False Creek Mouth.*

1965   Left U.B.C. and became writer-in-residence at Scarborough College of the University of Toronto.

1966-   *The Creative Writer* and *Selected Poems: 1940–1966*; writer-
1967   in-residence at Massey College, University of Toronto.

1967-   Writer-in-residence, University of Waterloo; *Memory No*
1968   *Servant* (Trumansburg, N.Y.); edited (with Margérie Lowry) *Lunar Caustic,* by Malcolm Lowry; awarded Canada Council Medal.

1968-   *The Poems of Earle Birney;* reading and lecturing tour of
1969   Australia and New Zealand on Canada Council Grant; *Pnomes, Jukollages and Other Stunzas.*

1971   *rag & bone shop.*

1972   *The Cow Jumped Over the Moon.*

1973   *what's so big about GREEN?* and *The Bear on the Delhi Road* (U.K.).

1975   *Collected Poems;* Awarded Canada Council Travelling Fellowship.

1976   *The Rugging and the Moving Times,* and *Alphabeings*

1977   *Ghost in the Wheels*

1978   *Fall by Fury.*

CHAPTER 1

Life and Times

I *Years of Preparation: 1904–1936*

EARLE Birney was born on 13 May 1904 in Calgary, now in the province of Alberta but at that time still in the North West Territories. His mother came from Shetland fisherfolk and crofters, and had worked as a waitress at a miner's hotel in the Kootenays. His father, the son of a small-town butcher, had run away from home at fifteen and drifted from California to Northern Alberta as "...a cowpuncher, brakeman, prospector [and] paper-hanger."[1] Earle's first seven years were spent on a remote farm between Calgary and Edmonton. He was an only child, and his isolation was accentuated by the fact that his father had to supplement the family income by working away from home in the winters, leaving Earle and his mother to take care of the farm. Some of the atmosphere of this life may be detected in "Joe Harris"; the visit of the crazy half-breed who is chased off by Joe's mother, wielding a shotgun, and the incident where Joe's father cuts his foot with an ax are based upon Birney's own experiences.[2]

Birney's lonely and isolated life was mitigated by the fact that his mother, who was exceptionally devout and who hoped that Earle would become a missionary, taught Sunday school in the settlement of Morningside, thereby also providing Earle with the opportunity to see other children and borrow books which he could read during the week. Both of Birney's parents were intensely aware of the benefits of education even though neither of them had completed elementary school, and even in his early years Earle was encouraged to read the Bible, *The Family Herald and Weekly Star,* and *Through Darkest Africa With Livingstone and Stanley.*[3] His mother also had a copy of Burns's *Poetical Works,* a courting gift from Earle's father, but being pious and teetotalling she had hid it from her son's youthful gaze. He discovered it and read it on the sly.

When Birney was seven his parents moved to Banff so that he might be close to school; there he was able to read Henty, Scott, Dumas, Captain Marryatt, and the nature stories of Charles G.D. Roberts.[4] The school had a fine curriculum that included Shakespeare, Poe, Hawthorne and the Romantic Poets even before Earle had reached grade nine.

In 1914 Birney's father held his mother to a promise she had made him when she had objected to his desire to fight in the Boer War in 1899, and enlisted for overseas service with the Canadian Army. He returned two years later shell-shocked and rheumatic. Since he was now incapable of working at his trade as a painter and paperhanger, he purchased a farm near Creston with the help of veterans' benefits but the farm was never really a success, and eventually the family moved once again, this time to Vancouver in order to be near Earle when he enrolled at the University of British Columbia in 1922.[5] Before this happened, however, Birney had to work for two years at a variety of manual jobs in order to earn the money for his university education. He later said that this two-year period as a laborer, from 1920 to 1922, temporarily delayed his development as a writer; he was deprived of books and culture and was exposed to ridicule when his coworkers learned that he indulged in writing poetry. Still, the experience of these years can be seen reflected in some of the poems he was to write later about working men.[6]

At the University of British Columbia Birney first enrolled in Arts with a view to eventually studying Engineering, it being the conventional wisdom, then as now, that engineers made more money than artsmen. But in his second year he took an extra English course and came under the influence of Garnett Sedgewick, a famous teacher. This, coupled with Birney's already long-established love of reading, was enough to cause him to switch to Honors English. He went on to become editor-in-chief of the university newspaper, the *Ubyssey,* and graduated in 1926 with first class honors. He was offered graduate fellowships by both Berkeley and Toronto and chose Toronto, where he took his Master of Arts degree in 1927, but when Toronto was unable to offer him another fellowship he did go to Berkeley, where he remained for the next three years working on his doctorate on Chaucer's irony and supporting himself as a teaching assistant. In the end, he was permanently barred from completing his doctorate at Berkeley by a new and inimical thesis director who felt that Birney's definition of irony was too broad, and that Birney resolutely refused to alter. Berkeley did help him to find a teaching job at the University of Utah, where he remained for two years.[7] In his poem "Once high upon a hill" Birney wrote of his engagement to a Berkeley girl, later broken, and of the beginning of the Depression, "...all that hasn't left me one good stink for savoring," but of the slave labor as a teaching assistant he does recall "sick smells of academia/its boardinghouses and its sweatshops and false scholars," things which he continued to denounce for the rest of his life.

In 1932 Birney returned to Toronto, where he completed the residence requirement for his doctorate. He also became involved in a Trotskyist group off campus, partly because one of its members was an extremely attractive girl, and in 1933 this group urged him to return to his job at Utah so that he could earn money for the cause and also to organize leftist protest groups. Birney went to Utah by way of Vancouver, where he had a summer teaching job. The next year Pelham Edgar, his director at the University of Toronto, got him a fellowship to complete his studies in England. Birney taught summer school for the sixth straight year at the University of British Columbia and then shipped out for England as an ordinary seaman on a British freighter sailing from Port Alberni.[8] The seven years Birney had just completed, struggling to survive and study as a teaching assistant, were an almost total loss in terms of creative output and help to explain his lack of poetic production during this period. Like all teaching assistants he was overworked and underpaid and given the most boring and onerous courses to teach. In these seven years he wrote only a few poems including "October in Utah." He was also kept back from writing poetry by the belief that artistic creation was a luxury to be deferred until after the revolution had established a socialist state: "I was so all-fired clear-cut political in the thirties that I regarded the writing of poetry as a treacherous withdrawal of energy from the class struggle." This theory, enunciated in Trotsky's *Literature and Revolution* (1924), gradually gave way to Birney's admiration for the left-wing verse of Auden, Spender, and Day Lewis, but for many years it served to stifle his poetic output.[9]

In England, Birney kept up his political activities within the Trotskyist faction of the Independent Labour party while researching and writing his doctoral thesis in the British Museum and the

University of London. He successfully completed his research and was awarded his degree by the University of Toronto in the spring of 1936 and was also appointed Lecturer in English in University College. Shortly after, he became literary editor of *Canadian Forum,* a journal with a socialist outlook devoted to literary and political commentary.

II *Years of Responsibility: 1936–1965*

Birney retained the editorship of *Canadian Forum* until 1940, although he actually continued supplying articles and reviews through 1941. When Germany invaded Russia in June 1941, Birney joined the Canadian Army, earning a commission in the reserve, and took leave of absence from the University of Toronto in 1942 to join the regular army. There was some question as to what to do with a man of his qualifications. Birney wanted to go to an infantry regiment; the armed forces countered with an offer of a job as an instructor on Link trainers, and the issue was finally resolved when Birney accepted a position as a Selection of Personnel Officer.

The outbreak of the war was, for Birney, a major turning point, especially as a writer. Up until 1940 he had written almost nothing; as he says himself, "Poems? In all that time scarcely a dozen, and nearly all trivia." Thus, he found himself at the age of thirty-five with no significant literary accomplishments in a familiar world that seemed about to disappear, and he began to write a few poems in a spirit of valediction to the years of peace, youth, and academe.[10] Although he says that up to this point he had thought of himself "as a scholar, critic, Marxist, potential novelist" but not as a poet, the writing of poetry was something he had had in mind for a long time; now, when pressure and opportunity combined, he wrote "David", "Dusk on English Bay", "Vancouver Lights", "Anglosaxon Street", and most of the other poems which were to appear in *David and Other Poems.*[11]

To begin with, Birney attempted to find a magazine that would print "David". After many rejections, he submitted the poem to *Canadian Forum,* but he did so with serious misgivings since he still had friends on the editorial staff and thought that such a gesture might not be cricket. Geoffrey Andrew accepted the poem for publication and Pelham Edgar subsequently encouraged Birney to submit a book of poems; this was the genesis of *David and Other Poems.*[12]

As A.J.M. Smith has observed, Birney's slim volume of twenty-one poems was something of a landmark in the history of Canadian letters. Up until the nineteen twenties Canadian poetry had been dominated, at least in part, by a tendency to imitate European models and sensibilities, to moralize and concern itself with the same philosophic issues that impinged upon the European conscience. Then, in the 1920s, taking their cue from the "new poets" in the United States and the Georgians in England, "...Canadian poets turned against rhetoric, sought a sharper, more objective imagery, and limited themselves as far as possible to the language of everyday rhythms of speech." If the new trend in Canadian poetry produced an occasionally harsher verse, it also incorporated images of farm, city, and industrial life that had hitherto been considered "unpoetic" but which were nonetheless recognizably Canadian in their origin. The movement, led by Dorothy Livesay, Raymond Knister, Anne Marriott, Louis Dudek, and Raymond Souster, culminated in a sense in Birney's *David and Other Poems,* which "...combined a cosmopolitan sensibility and an adventurous technique with a thoroughly native pride in what is excellent and unique in Canadian life." Birney sums up the new movement by combining pride in the beauties of Canadian life with disgust and shame at the filth and social inequities that mar this beauty.[13] To this, one should add the observation that "...part of the book's favourable reception was due to its timeliness. Birney's immersion in political events in the thirties is evident in both the concerns of the book and the way it captures the mood of a nation going reluctantly to war."[14]

The truth of this last remark can be observed in poems like "Hands," which opens in a manner reminiscent of Lampman's "Morning on the *Lièvre*":

> In the amber morning by the inlet's high shore
> My canoe drifts and the slim trees come bending
> Arching the palms of their still green hands
> Juggling the shimmer of ripples....

Here Birney links his observation of nature to a political commentary on the world scene. Where Lampman would probably have been content to note the similarity between human hands and those of the cedars, Birney makes sure that we understand the irony implicit in that similarity:

Cold and unskilled is the cedar, his webbed claws
Drooping over the water shall focus no-bombsight
Nor suture the bayoneted bowel....

This is an early poem, but it contains many of Birney's permanent preoccupations, including a profound love of the natural world, the loneliness of the human situation, a satirical disgust at mankind's follies, and even, in the reference to "...the wrinkled / Index weaving the virtuous sock..." his pervasive sense of mythology.

Moreover, perhaps the enthusiasm with which *David and Other Poems* was received was due to the fact that the war lent even greater significance to the title poem. Perhaps Canadians responded to the young man who was ready to die for his ideals, and in a sense David's greatest ideal was liberty: he chose death rather than the confinement of a wheelchair. The subsequent horrors of the war, including Belsen, Auschwitz, and Hiroshima may have had the effect of diminishing the pathos of the quick, brutal death of one brave youth, but in 1942 David could still be seen as the heroic leader: competent, tough, brave, knowledgeable and good-natured. He is also very nearly Christlike in his acceptance of guilt: "No, Bobbie! Don't ever blame yourself. / I didn't test my foothold," and responsibility: "I'd do it [i.e., kill] for you, Bob." Canadians, with a new war on their hands, must have felt as inexperienced and dismayed as Bob, and it is not surprising that this poem of David and his mountains, each in their way fatalistic and calm, should have held such an appeal for them.

In this volume there also appeared "Vancouver Lights," a poem which must be considered remarkable in the Birney canon. While it evokes once again the sense that infuses so many of the other poems of fear and uncertainty in the face of war, it is still unique in being one of the few poems Birney ever wrote that expresses any sort of pride or satisfaction in the human race and its accomplishments. Although in the course of the poem Birney acknowledges the fact that war is a manmade disease capable of rendering fearful and dangerous even such a beautiful element as light — "Now through the feckless years we have come to the time / when to look on this quilt of lamps is a troubling delight" — he does conclude on a remarkably laudatory note. Having reviewed all the foreseeable horrors that await mankind, he says:

This must we say,

Whoever may be to hear us, if the murk devour,
and none weave again in gossamer:

These rays were ours,

we made and unmade them. Not the shudder of continents
doused us, the moon's passion, nor crash of comets.
In the fathomless heat of our dwarfdom, our dream's
combustion,
we contrived the power, the blast that snuffed us.
No one slew Prometheus. Himself he chained
and consumed his own bright liver. O stranger,
Plutonian, descendant, or beast in the night —
    there was light.

By any standard, *David and Other Poems* had to be counted a success. E. J. Pratt referred to the "hearty acceptance of this volume by literary critics and general readers," although he did also say that some of the shorter poems were marked by a dry over-compression, "a cryptic virtue which may so easily pass into mannerism...."[15] Birney also received a note from Sir Charles G. D. Roberts praising "David" (unfortunately Sir Charles also praised "On Going to the Wars," the weakest poem in the collection), and the book won the Governor General's Poetry Award for 1942. Still, ironies abounded in a profusion that must have delighted Birney's sardonic soul; after struggling to get the volume published and reviewed and after winning such recognition with his first work, Birney found the publisher unwilling to bring out a second edition in the spring of 1943 because he knew that Birney was going overseas and thought he might not be coming back to produce anything else.[16]

As it turned out, Birney's wartime service proved in some ways to be a blessing since it exposed him to a vast variety of people and places, relieved him of the tedium of teaching, gave him an adequate salary for the first time in his life, and allowed him plenty of time to write and think.[17] His experiences in the training camps in Canada, in wartime England, and in northwestern Europe were to provide a rich fund of experience on every level; more specifically, Birney's work as a Selection of Personnel Officer obliged him to become an "amateur psychologist," to enquire closely into and try to understand the reasons underlying a wide variety of human actions and emotions. He had to assess and counsel men who wanted to become paratroopers or cooks or tank drivers or conscientious objectors. Birney absorbed this rich experience and spent his ample spare time in the preparation of the poems that were to appear in his next book, *Now Is Time*.

The poems in this book, which appeared in 1945, are grouped in sections subtitled "Tomorrow," "Yesterday," and "Today," groupings which serve to underline the theme implicit in the title, i.e., now is the time to decide whether or not mankind is to survive. This theme is stated explicitly in "World Conference," the last poem in the book:

> The compassed mind must quiver north
>   though every chart defective;
> there is no fog but in the will,
>   the iceberg is elective.

As for the subsections themselves, the "Tomorrow" section includes poems both urgent and somber on the topic of what will happen if a permanent peace is not established; those in the "Yesterday" section are reminders of what the war was really like; and the three poems which compose the "Today" group concentrate upon the possibility of mankind taking positive action to cure the ills which beset it. If Birney is not openly optimistic in these poems, he is at least hopeful. In the "Tomorrow" section he had deliberately counterbalanced the gloomy "Remarks for the Part of Death" on page four with the affirmations in "Lines for a Peace" on the facing page:

> While shadow-seconds race our sea
> below the milky waves of might
> the mind says yes and yes and Be
> and beautiful the fisted light.
>
> . . . .
>
> The hours flash below the sun
> and space is now and now is time
> to bed the beast and with the pain
> of love shock him to the brain—
> then certify the future sane.

Similarly, the last three poems in the book, "Death of a War," which asserts that "Still the heart is a metal vibrant / to love in his lightning searches"; "Young Veterans," which notes that "Hates like souvenirs are thumbed awhile / then lost in moving or by the playing child''; and ''World Conference,'' cited above, all suggest that perhaps man may at last have learned how to avoid his more destructive impulses. The critics were quick to observe this aspect of Birney's new work. George Herbert Clarke noted, ''If in some of his verses wry or bitter words appear they quickly merge with the widening themes of hope and growth, the departure from dead selves toward higher things,''[18] and M. H. Martin felt that ''...a considered mature optimism is the background of the most serious poems in this book.''[19]

On the other hand, some critics once again commented upon the obscurity of some of the poems in this book. ''Skeleton in Grass,'' aside from being a dismal *memento mori,* is certainly one of the most cryptic poems Birney ever published. Watson Kirkconnel went even further, saying that the book as a whole was disappointing because of the obscurity in which many of the poems were hidden. He singled out a passage in ''On a Diary'' as an example of something that would be intelligible only to readers of Hardy's *Return of the Native.*[20] It is true that this poem needed a good deal of reworking, mainly because Birney lost control of the initial governing image of a tree growing and developing as a metaphor for the development of a girl into a woman, but, as we shall see farther on, it did contain the elements of what was to become a very fine poem. Aside from combining the best aspects of his later philosophical poems like ''The Bear on the Delhi Road'' it also falls into the tradition of his long narrative poems like ''David,'' ''Four Feet Between,'' and ''The Gray Woods Exploding'' in the sense that it is a profound reflection upon the interreactions of man with society and man with nature. More important, it was the best and subtlest treatment of women and love to appear in Birney's work for many years. Nearly a quarter of a century was to pass before Birney dealt with the subject of women with the grave courtesy that infuses ''On a Diary.''

The whole question of obscurity in Birney's work is a complicated one. From the very outset of his poetic career he had publicly announced that he was trying to avoid the ''fashionable obscurity'' of the writers of the 1930s like Eliot and Auden and to write in a simple, lucid style accessible to all intelligent people. One can only suggest that at this stage of his development his technique was not the equal of his aspirations. Another contributing factor might have been his own quick intelligence, which presumed a similar acuity on the part of the reader and thus led him to use too elliptical a style. Perhaps the most important factor is that Birney is an intensely private man. Underlying the gregarious, globe-trotting public figure one constantly senses the existence of a man who is careful not to reveal too much of himself. Occasionally, in poems like "The Road to Nijmegen,"

> ...this road that arrives at no future,
>   for this guilt
> in the griefs of the old and the graves of the young,

Birney exorcises some agony or sense of personal guilt he has experienced over the mess the world is in, a mess which seems to derive from man's competition with man and nature but often enough, especially in his early works, he hides behind a manner that is bantering or ironic or unfortunately vague.

Despite these criticisims, *Now Is Time* also won the Governor General's Award for Poetry, and Birney went to work for the Canadian Broadcasting Corporation in Montreal. He was employed as a supervisor of foreign-language broadcasts to Europe for the International Service, where he was "responsible for making sure that Canadian foreign policy was accurately reflected in the broadcasts."[21] After a year of this, he left to accept a teaching appointment at the University of British Columbia. The conditions were primitive, the teaching load heavy, and the classes jammed with returned soldiers studying on veterans' benefits. Despite this, Birney found time in the summer of 1947 to write enough poems for another book, *Strait of Anian,* which was published in 1948.

In fact, *Strait of Anian* contained only twenty-two new poems; the rest had appeared in his two previous volumes. In part, the publisher followed this practice of reprinting poems because it was cheaper than keeping the original volumes in print. It also made the purchaser think he was getting more for his money. But in some cases, notably that of "David," poems were reprinted because they contributed to that part of *Strait of Anian* which illustrated the physical and cultural scope of Canada.[22] The section entitled "One Society" begins with "Atlantic Door" and works westward via "New Brunswick," "Quebec May," "Prairie Counterpoint," and so on, until it comes to a close with "Pacific Door," which, incidentally, ends with the same three lines as "Atlantic Door." As an epigraph to this section Birney chose Wordsworth's lines:

> ...There is a dark
> Inscrutable workmanship that reconciles
> Discordant elements, making them cling together
> In one society

and it is clear that he was attempting to illustrate Canada's common experience of itself as a country, just as he was trying in the second section, entitled "One World," to show that Canada shared a common set of hopes and problems with the other nations of the world. The title of the book is taken from Thomas Blundeville's account of Sir Francis Drake's first voyage to the Indies and refers to his sailors' unwillingness to press the search for the northwest passage, "the narrow sea Anian." The implication is that mankind as a whole would have to press *its* search for a passage, however narrow, cold, and dangerous, out of the perils that were besetting the world in 1948:

> the problem that is ours and yours
> that there is no clear Strait of Anian
> to lead us easy back to Europe,
> that men are isled in ocean or in ice
> and only joined by long endeavour to be joined.
> ("Pacific Door," ll. 19–23)

Yet, if Birney felt that mankind had a perilous passage ahead he was still reasonably optimistic about the future. In an article published in 1946 he had referred to "this desperately sick but curable world."[23] Perhaps the pessimism and ironic contempt for human folly that was eventually to become characteristic of Birney's poetry had been temporarily nullified by the euphoria of having participated in the winning of a "just" war, in seeing a promise of prosperity and employment for all and in the hope that a new social order could be established. To be sure, poems like "Remarks for the Part of Death" reflect Birney's generally gloomy reaction to the war, and "VE-Night" is a commentary on mankind's cynical ability to forget the horrors of war:

> ...here's a bob for balmy dreams that pass.
> We've saved the soppy world again
> don't nag tonight with what we saved it for,

but these are counterbalanced by lines like those in the elegy for
Birney's friend, the poet Steve Cartwright:

> Since you who walked in freedom and the ways of reason
> fought on our front, we foresee the plot is solvable,
> the duel worthy.

If Birney could ask dubiously in "Canada: Case History," "will
[Canada] learn to grow up before it's too late?" he could also let
himself go in an exuberant celebration of life and youth in "Quebec
May." Similarly, he counterbalanced his depressing memories of
"a nursery of crosses abroad" and his misgivings about man, who
is

> a snow that cracks
> the trees' red resinous arches
> and winters the cabined heart

in "Man is a Snow" with his reference in the companion poem,
"...or a Wind," to "the great wind of humanity blowing free
blowing through / streaming over the future." Furthermore, he
chose the same closing poem for this volume as he had for *Now Is
Time.* "World Conference" is an expression of a certain faith in
common sense and the human intellect, which suggests that two
years after the war had ended Birney still retained some optimism
about the future.

One critic also commented upon the "Wider variety, greater
maturity and increased technical competence"[24] of Birney's work
in *Strait of Anian.* His reworking of "Dusk on English Bay" from
David and Other Poems could be taken as an example of these
qualities. In *Strait of Anian* he changed the title to simply "Dusk
on the Bay," thereby implying that the observer in the poem could
be standing on the shore of any bay anywhere in the world. Also,
the formal capitalization and punctuation of the early version gives
way in *Strait of Anian* to a less formal, more cursive style, just as
all of Birney's poetry was eventually to become freer as he aban-
doned punctuation almost entirely and replaced it with shaped
stanzas and breathing spaces to indicate not only the pauses but
even the theme and the mood of his poems.

With his standing as a poet now recognized widely throughout
Canada and in Great Britain, Birney turned to the writing of a

novel based upon his own experiences before and during the war. *Turvey* is the story of a former drifter who joins the Canadian Army in 1942. His misadventures during basic training in Canada, in England, and eventually on the Continent are linked by his attempts to have himself posted to the Kootenay Highlanders, a unit from his own home region and the regiment in which his best friend, Mac, is serving. He manages to catch up with the regiment near the Rhine in the winter of 1944, only to find that Mac has just been killed. Turvey comes down with diphtheria and is evacuated to England and finally invalided home; before he leaves England, however, he manages to become engaged to an English girl who promises to follow him to Canada. Throughout his career in the army Turvey's *bête noir* is the Selection of Personnel Officer, who reappears in various places and in various guises to torment Turvey with a series of IQ and aptitude tests. Turvey himself, although he is not very bright, is strong, loyal, affectionate, easygoing, and, compared to the SPOs, fairly well balanced. The intellectual powers aside, there is much of Birney himself in the character of Turvey: most of Turvey's experiences with injuries, illness, and military hospitals were drawn from firsthand experience;[25] Turvey also reflects Birney's own proletarian background and outlook, his detestation of jargon, his wide variety of prewar jobs, his disgust with the reality of war, and his ironic tendency to see himself as fate's plaything.

Although *Turvey* did provide a means for Birney to record his wartime experiences, the novel also had a more serious and practical purpose. Birney hoped to make enough money through its sales to liberate himself from the necessity of earning his living in the teaching profession; he once said that he would never write anything as popular as *Turvey* again, and did not want to.[26] This seems to indicate that by the summer of 1947 he saw himself as a poet by vocation and that every other money-making activity was henceforth to be only a means by which he could buy time to pursue his career as a poet. With this concept clear in his mind for what was probably the first time, he took a month in the summer of 1947 and wrote the first chapter of *Turvey* in a hideaway on Bowen Island. The following summer he completed the first draft, writing sometimes at the rate of 5,000 words per day.[27]

After much revision, and a savage bowdlerizing at the insistence of the editors, Turvey was finally published in 1949. In the first few years after its appearance critical reaction was mixed; one writer remarked that it tended to disintegrate into a series of *fabliaux* about army life and, with more justification, that no Canadian, living or dead, had ever talked like Turvey's friend Mac.[28] One CBC reviewer said he did not think he would want his daughter to read it (if he had a daughter); *Turvey* was banned in several Ontario libraries; another critic complained of its "Rabelaisian" quality.[29] To this catalogue of sins one might add that *Turvey* contained the earliest examples of what was to become a pervasive and annoying aspect of Birney's attitude toward non-English-speaking people: his tendency to overrate their moral and intellectual abilities vis-à-vis those of the "northamerican." *Turvey* contains two portraits of French Canadians, one of whom is a hero from Dieppe and both of whom make their Anglophone counterparts look weak, sniveling, and inept by comparison.

Despite such adverse commentary, *Turvey* sold well in Canada. Its most ardent admirers were old sweats of all ranks and all services who found in it a true-to-life chronicle of their own adventures and misadventures in the service.[30] However, the British publishers at first rejected it as being too American in its humor, and the Americans refused it on the grounds that it was too British; thus *Turvey* became a factual example of the Canadian stereotype.[31] Eventually, in 1959 an edition was brought out in Great Britain. The British also paid Birney the ultimate compliment of bringing out a pirated version in 1960 under the title of *The Kootenay Highlander.* Finally, the novel was adapted as a stage play. It ran for seven weeks in Toronto and for a full season as musical comedies in two different theaters,[32] but even in this Birney was dogged by bad luck; the Toronto version had been scooped by the appearance of *No Time for Sergeants* on Broadway,[33] and the production at the Charlottetown Festival in the summer of 1966 did not achieve the success of the traditional *Anne of Green Gables* because of the horror of the island's Grundies at its supposed obscenities.[34] Since that time, however, the novel has been recognized as a Canadian classic and has sold steadily year after year.

For the next three summers Birney worked on a radio play in verse and a selection of poems that was to appear in 1952 as *Trial of a City and Other Verse. Trial of a City,* among other things, reflects Birney's long-standing relationship with the city of Vancouver. In articles and poems published over nearly a quarter of a century, he expresses the dilemma of a sensitive man admiring on the one hand the glorious mountain and ocean setting of Vancouver, while on the other hand he despairs at the tawdriness of its architecture and the Babbittry of its inhabitants. In this play, the city is on trial for these and other sins. The question posed by the "Office of the Future" in the "Ministry of History" is whether or not the city should be obliterated because of its grossness, ugliness, pollution, political corruption, and philistinism. The city is defended, rather ineptly, by a man named Legion who is only capable of expressing himself in tourist-brochure clichés, while the prosecution is led by Gabriel Powers, who is capable of calling up from the past and then dematerializing at will a series of damning witnesses: Captain George Vancouver, a long-dead headman of the Salish Indian tribe, a geology professor from the university, "Gassy Jack" Deighton, and William Langland. Powers, the attorney with the archangelic name and Faustian attributes, has no difficulty in demonstrating that in fact the city should be wiped from the face of the earth, but just when the situation seems hopeless a surprise witness, Mrs. Anyone, appears for the defense and demands to be heard. Invoking mainly existential arguments, she reconciles the Future to the fact of the city of Vancouver and wins a reprieve. Judgment is suspended *sine die.*

The play as a condemnation of Vancouver and of Western civilization in general is well structured, largely because the facts of Vancouver's ghastliness are all too obvious, but the blanket condemnation of the present in favor of the past, although holding a powerful appeal for romantics and nature lovers, is unconvincing. For example, Langland's implication that the modern city represents the antithesis of a better moral and physical order ignores the unpleasant facts of plague, illiteracy, simony, famine, and serfdom which were the commonplaces of his own age. Also, the sudden reversal of the gloomy conclusion toward which the enquiry is drawing is too pat. Mrs. Anyone, the Earth-Mother, invokes such existential arguments as "I live, damnation is not now" and "Without my longer Will, my stubborn boon, / You'd have no mate to check with but the cornered moon. / It's my defiant fear keeps green my whirling world," and the heretofore glib and omniscient Mr. Powers is checkmated. One has the impression that Birney, while trying to reflect the apocalyptic sense of the early years of the Cold War and the McCarthy hearings, turns out to be a cheerful humanitarian. In many ways, this basic tension was to characterize much of Birney's work; his private vision of doom has always had to struggle against his own good nature and a certain

western-Canadian expansiveness. Like Swift, he has often elo-
quently expressed his distaste for mankind at large but he cannot
bring himself to wish that every human being whom he knows and
loves as an individual might be blown to hell. In *Trial of a City,* as
in *Turvey,* the undercurrent of sorrow, malignancy, and despair is
kept in check by the good-natured common man.

Contemporary reviewers of *Trial of a City* were quick to comment upon the weak and unconvincing ending of the play, where
the city's deserved condemnation ''...is suspended on grounds
whose humanitarian and theological propriety cannot conceal or
redeem the sentimentality of the presentation or the brusque reversal of the poem's mood...,''[35] and the "unconvincing" nature of
Mrs. Anyone's argument.[36] They also noted Birney's use of
Joycean word-play and the fact that, like Joyce in *Ulysses,* Birney
ran through a gamut of earlier literary styles. In fact, Birney did
put on an impressive display of verbal foolery and doubletalk as
well as switching his style from the frivolous to the serious as circumstances and the nature of the speaker demanded, but this display of technical versatility is not the saving grace of the poem any
more than is its rather weak plot. What has maintained the esteem
of Birney's readers over the years is actually the lyrical quality of
many of the speeches in the play. Captain George Vancouver is circumspect and judicious as a good navigator must be and William
Langland is suitably astringent, but Birney's *coup de maître* resides
in his portrayal of the Salish Chief. In words that are dignified,
gentle, and inexpressibly poignant by turns, the old chief relates the
joys of his youth, the customs of his people, and their ultimate
destruction by the intrusion of the white man. In the face of yap-
ping Legion he gently recalls the time when

> Comfort was in the dogwool shirt of my youth,
> the tassels of flying squirrel
> tailing like smoke from my shoulders,
> not the trader's cast-offs in my aging.
> Comfort was the winter's bear-haunches safe in the rafters,
> when as a child I darted laughing under the reed handings,
> with a little fist of hazelnuts clutched from the cedar chest.
> Comfort was waking beside my wife
> on our bed of musk-sweet rushes.

The speech of the Salish Chief is certainly one of the best poems that Birney ever wrote, and in some ways it therefore upstages the thirteen lyrics which form the second part of this book. Of these, two are in part technological dividends from Birney's year with the Canadian Broadcasting Corporation; "Christmas Comes" and "North Star West" reflect the knowledge of electronics he acquired during that year. Two others, "The Monarch of the Id" and "Restricted Area," are satires directed at literary censorship in Canada and anti-Semitism, and the remainder are upon a variety of topics from ecology to neurosis to human love. Two important factors are worth noting about this collection and about the book as a whole: with *Trial of a City and Other Verse* Birney left World War II firmly behind and was now preoccupied with contemporary matters. These matters, however, were not necessarily less alarming than had been the war or the Depression; *Trial of a City and Other Verse* only marks the point where Birney ceases to be preoccupied with the immediate fact of a real war and begins to contemplate deeply the depression and anxiety of the Cold War and the seemingly limitless folly of a human race determined to destroy the world in which it lives.

By this time, Birney had "become one of the best-known men of letters in the Dominion,"[37] sharing "the interest of the Group of the Sixties in the landscape of Canada, the interest of Pratt in narrative poetry and in human fidelity and courage, [and] the interest of the Montreal Group in verse technique, social satire and political action."[38] The significance of his contribution to Canadian letters not only in the field of poetry but also as an editor, fiction-writer, teacher, and critic was cited by Roy Daniells when he nominated Birney for the Lorne Pierce Medal of the Royal Society of Canada in 1952. Daniells also noted that the medal was traditionally awarded to the Canadian author "whose critical or creative writing notably succeeds in interpreting Canadian life to the Canadian people."[39] In the ten short years since Birney had made his debut with *David and Other Poems* he had become a nationally known literary figure and, more unusual in Canadian literature, a poet who was not associated solely with one region. Birney had always striven to comprehend and express the totality of Canada just as he was to attempt in his future works to illustrate the unity of all human beings, for good or ill, in every part of the world.

As it happened, Birney was not on hand to accept personally the honor proffered by the Royal Society; he had received an overseas

fellowship from the Canadian government and was on his way by
freighter to France for a year, where he would write his second
novel, *Down the Long Table*. This novel is the story of a young college instructor, Gordon Saunders, struggling toward a doctorate in
English literature in the midst of the Depression. He teaches for a
time in Salt Lake City and later studies at the University of
Toronto. While in Salt Lake City he has an affair with the wife of a
professor. His mistress later dies as a result of an attempted abor-
tion. While Saunders is in Toronto he accidentally becomes involved with the Communist party and goes to the local meetings
more out of curiosity than anything else. He later joins the Trotskyist faction and becomes engaged to an empty-headed girl whose
mother's house is the site of the Trotskyist meetings. His political
mentors convince him to go to "organize Vancouver" during the
summer of 1933 before returning to Salt Lake City. Saunders
crosses Canada on freight trains, lives in a flophouse in Vancouver,
and manages to organize a "cadre" of four Trotskyites, one of
whom is a police informer. His fiancée writes from Toronto to tell
him that she is marrying someone else, his cadre is broken up by the
police and rejected by the main Trotskyite groups in New York and
Toronto. The police informer is killed by another member of the
cadre and Saunders is helped to flee Vancouver by one of his former professors at the University of British Columbia. He later com-
pletes his doctoral studies, achieves success in academe, and
becomes an American citizen. As the book closes, though, he is
preparing to answer the questions of a McCarthy-style committee
into his activities in the 1930s.

The novel is characterized by verbosity, intense political naiveté
on the part of its characters, a sense of despair which was becoming
more and more typical of Birney regarding the inability of any individual to help any other individual, and a certain cynicism about
human motives. The verbosity manifests itself in passages like the
following description of Gordon Saunders:

He is ... yellow-curled, though no darling; a mixture perhaps of all; of
the scholastic child in his coiled cherubic head and his air of being con-
cerned with some inner conversation; of the Elizabethan man in the supple
enquiring length of his nose and the sensual flare of his nostril and lip; of
the wandering soldier in the unexpected thrust of his jaw and the set of his
muscular shoulders; of the messiah, and the fool, in the lifted half-seeing
gaze of his great deer's eyes,[40]

and the political naiveté is evident in the belief, for example, that one youth, who as yet had not even grasped Marx's concept of the dialectic, could organize a city the size of Vancouver in a few weeks' time and in the face of fierce opposition by the police, the government, and local political factions. As Ralph Fox, a British left-wing writer who was killed in the Spanish Civil War, once remarked, "The least credible figures in the novels written about revolutions are the revolutionaries."[41]

On the other hand, the despairing sense of the loneliness of the individual and the suspicions about most people's political motives gives rise to one of the outstanding symbolic figures in the book: Ole Hansen, an old logger, who in the end rejects communism, Trotskyism, everything, to form a one-man party based on his belief in his own uniqueness and worth, and on the belief that things can be better. If he does manage to work out a better system men will come to him. As he says, "Lenin was alone once, [too]."[42] The note of combined optimism and despair upon which the book ends is also a function of Birney's growing belief at that time that although no political party or dogma would serve to heal and unite mankind, yet all men are alike and, in fact, one in their search for a social order better than that which has been created so far. In place of political parties, Birney, and Saunders, came to believe mainly in the creative and poetic nature of man however diverse those manifestations may be; to be a man and to struggle is to be a poet in some sense.

One critic observed that certain chapters of *Down the Long Table* are set in dramatic dialogue, a technique employed by James Joyce in *Ulysses,* and that also as in *Ulysses* certain literary quotations are repeated as keynote phrases for each major character or situation.[43] Another noted Birney's use of snippets of contemporary news items and headlines to set the tone of certain sections of *Down the Long Table.* While it is true that this technique obviously had been borrowed from Dos Passos's *U.S.A.* and that Birney had previously used it in his "Rufus" columns in the *Canadian Forum* in the late 1930s,[44] in this case he may have been prompted to resurrect it by the fact that he had recently been giving some radio talks on popular semantics and he had wanted to start "a weekly column of the air with commentary leading up to each week's use and abuse of words of emotional significance, culled from the press, radio and movies."[45]

As for the topicality of the novel, the direct and obvious links with McCarthy witch-hunts which made one reviewer suspect, "...that the author is trying to gloss over his hero's moral failures, and that he is depending on his reader's antipathy to McCarthyism to secure sympathy for a character who does not deserve it,"[46] Birney conceded that this had been a mistake. When the 1975 paperback reissue of the novel was in preparation he tried unsuccessfully to have the publisher drop the opening and closing scenes which take place at a Senate Investigating Committee hearing.[47] In spite of these considerations, *Down the Long Table* is in many ways superior to *Turvey*. In it Birney moved away from *Turvey's* loose, episodic style and experimented with a considerable range of prose techniques. Gordon Saunders is a much more subtly and fully developed character than Turvey; he may be naive and an intellectual snob, but at least he is a recognizable human being, whereas Turvey tended to be a composite of familiar army types. Finally, the much greater length and complexity of *Down the Long Table* showed that Birney had developed as a novelist to the point where he could sustain and work out a serious theme.

After the appearance of *Down the Long Table* Birney published very little for several years; in fact, his next volume of poetry, *Ice Cod Bell or Stone,* only appeared in 1962, ten years after the publication of *Trial of a City*. It is true that his teaching schedule was as heavy as ever and that he did spend a year from 1958 to 1959 in England doing research on a book on Chaucer and that at times he suffered much difficulty from a painful inflamation of the eyes,[48] but even when these factors are taken into account the fact remains that between 1953 and 1957 he seems to have written only seventeen new poems.[49] One critic attributed Birney's silence to a general sense of discouragement with the state of society and the mess the world as a whole seemed to be in.[50] There seems to be considerable validity in this view; Birney noted in a gloomy article composed in "the tenth year of the Atomic Age" that most of the recent graduates of his creative-writing courses had simply quit writing, not because they were unable to find publishers but because "...they ... lost faith not so much in their own ability to create as in the world's ability to enjoy." In the same article he says that "...the really typical problem of writers emerging in the years since Hiroshima is the problem of a growth of a doubt, a condition of *accidia,* of spiritual dryness, an attitude of defeatism regarding man's fate, which reflects itself in a negation of the importance of writing ... as a medium of art."[51] To these considerations may be added the observation made by John Sutherland in 1951 when he claimed that although the war had been a tremendous stimulus to Canadian poetry, the end of the war brought the realization that Russia and the West were at loggerheads. Since the new poets of the 1940s had strong political motivations, this realization along with the knowledge that the Canadian socialist movement had very shallow roots disillusioned many of them and made them turn to other interests. Sutherland said that Birney's contemporaries "...no longer attribute the present state of the world to class oppression, but to a guilt which makes no class distinctions and which involves every individual, including the poet."[52]

Gradually, the depressing images of the nuclear age crept into Birney's writing. Even a lightheartedly satirical defense of creative-writing courses has a passage full of references to Distant Early Warning lines, interceptors, lead-lined shelters, and radioactivity,[53] and in a major poem, "November Walk Near False Creek Mouth," written in 1961, the imagery of nuclear destruction is all-pervasive. Beginning with the first three lines: "The time is the last of the warmth / and the fading of brightness / before the final flash and the night" the motif is echoed two stanzas later: "they come to the last innocent warmth / and the fading / before the unimaginable brightness" and is repeated in nearly every subsequent stanza of the nine-page poem. There are references to "...the days of the separate wait / for the mass dying," and specific allusions to the effects of the Hiroshima blast:

> Outward the sun   explodes light
> like a mild rehearsal of light to come
> over the vitreous waters
> At this edge of the blast
> a young girl sits on a granite bench
> so still as if already only
> silhouette burned in the stone

and to the "...strata of jetstreams / the air-roads [that] wait the two-way traffic [of rockets]." To reinforce the gloomy atmosphere of nuclear peril, Birney also comments upon the other ways in which man and nature have conspired to destroy the planet upon which we live. He refers to "...the shapeless town / and its dying shapers," the "...almost / immortal ocean at work / on the earth's liquidation," to "the manstruck forest," "the doomed

whales," "the cooling sun," and to "...the vanishing squirrel /
and the spilling city."

Considering all these elements, it could reasonably be argued
that Birney lost all faith in organized political parties sometime in
the early 1950s. Like Joe Harris he had always demanded "a creed,
not a dogma," but now he seems to have come to believe that mankind as a whole was incapable of using reason to master its baser
instincts. Coupled with this depressing conclusion, and contributing to it, were the facts of nuclear proliferation and ecological
destruction. "November Walk Near False Creek Mouth" is the
summing up of many of these preoccupations. Birney was to deal
with them again many times in his subsequent poems, often with a
shrill satire that descended into vituperation, but at least by the late
1950s he had managed to master, if not reconcile himself to, his
gloomy view of the world and was writing poetry again. Out of the
poems produced in this period was to come his finest single volume
of verse.

Ice Cod Bell or Stone, which appeared in 1962, reveals Birney at
his very best in the sense that the poems deal with a set of interests
that literally range around the world and reach both backward and
forward in time. Moreover, the tone of this work taken as a whole
is remarkably balanced and consistent, avoiding especially the vituperation and despair that were to disfigure some of his later poems
in books like *rag & bone shop* and *what's so big about GREEN?*
Also, in this volume Birney dispensed with the rather artificial geographical and thematic groupings of poems that he had employed
in *Strait of Anian* and *Trial of a City,* in favor of a loose, unobtrusive association of poems that examine a series of places and
themes. In the words of Frank Davey, "In [*Ice Cod Bell or Stone*]
Birney's fondness for generalizing has become a fondness for particular people and scenes, even for anecdotes.... His desire for
overview [of Canada and its problems] has dissolved into a town-
by-town investigation of rural Mexico.... Rhetoric has for the
most part yielded to conversational diction and rhythms ... which
seem certain progeny of the colloquial *Turvey* and [*Trial of a
City*]."[54] In other words, *Ice Cod Bell or Stone* marks the point at
which Birney ceased to be preoccupied mainly with Canadian
themes and began to take the whole world as the source of his
experience.

The reasons for Birney's expanded approach to the world and its
problems derive in part from his experiences in the 1950s. He made

several trips to Mexico and on his way to England in 1958 he had gone via the Pacific, India, and the Middle East. This had provided him with a rich fund of observations about the nature of human-kind as a whole and about the world in general. Also, in his article dealing with the dilemma of the writer in the nuclear age he had concluded by saying, "Perhaps the very sharpness of the hope-despair conflict in these times has meant the throwing up of a par-ticularly rich confusion of ideas and of attempts to systematize them."[55] The combination of these two factors — exposure to alien cultures and the stimulus of anxiety — seems to underlie the bal-anced, thoughtful catholicity of the poems in *Ice Cod Bell or Stone*.

To appreciate the scope of the poems in this book one must real-ize that they literally take the reader around the world, from Van-couver to Hawaii to Japan to India, to Greece, and to Spain. They make him follow a track that leads up and down the North Ameri-can continent from the Arctic to Mexico. And they move freely through time as well, back through the exploits of Cook and Bering, past considerations of the Cruxifixion in "El Greco: Espolio" to the Orpheus myth encapsuled in "Pachucan Miners," and forward to the fate of man and society in "Answers to a Grade-School Biology Test":

> *Have* [rats] *any use for science?*
>   For their own science, yes;
>   under the streets they think and multiply
>   till men have cleared themselves and cats
>   from all the earth that glares at sky,
>   and there is freedom to preside, for rats,

and in the poem "Ellesmereland," from which the title of the vol-ume is drawn:

> No man is settled on that coast
> The harebells are alone
> Nor is there talk of making man
> from ice cod bell or stone.

Within this far-ranging framework of time and space Birney deals with an equally broad variety of themes and emotions. One sees heroic explorers cheek by jowl with babbling yahoos, young chil-dren with old trees, satire with social commentary, laughter with depression. In "Ellesmereland" one sees Birney's cynical attitude toward the human race beginning to emerge, and "Appeal to a Lady with a Diaper" is one of his very earliest, and best, attempts at concrete poetry. In later volumes the cynicism would often degenerate into invective and the use of concrete form into mannerism, but in *Ice Cod Bell or Stone* all these disparate elements are muted, balanced, and controlled in a work of highest skill and maturity.

In 1962 Birney obtained a grant from the Canada Council to conduct a reading tour through the Caribbean and parts of South America. The experiences of this trip, which lasted for several months, were transmuted into a series of poems which, along with some poems reprinted from previous volumes, appeared under the title *Near False Creek Mouth* in 1964. The book is actually a rather haphazard collection of poems grouped roughly around the Caribbean, the West Coast and Western South America, various parts of Europe, and Canada. Each section, beginning with "Caribbean Turnabout" is prefaced by a sketch map of the area in question; each map also shows the geographic relationship of the area to False Creek Mouth (or Vancouver). The last section, subtitled "Near False Creek Mouth," has a map which includes most of the major points of interest in Birney's peregrinations: Machu Picchu, Santiago de Chile, Buenos Aires, the Caribbean, London, Madrid, Budapest, Epidaurus, and back to False Creek Mouth via Wolfville, Nova Scotia, and Hamilton, Ontario. The implications, the same ones that Birney was trying to make as far back as 1948 in *Strait of Anian,* are that we all live near False Creek Mouth even though we may be "farthest neighbours" and that the poet's efforts serve in part to remind us of this fact.

This motif is borne out by poems like "Transistor." Birney has been taken by a sound-engineer interested in recording folk music back into the hills of Jamaica. There, a tiny, wizened woman grasping a twig broom sings from memory the airs that reach back through four generations of her people's history:

> ...all the way
> back to the sea and the canebrakes
> her greatgrandfather ran from
> the night he brought her words
> stored in his rebellious head
> beyond the howl of the slavers hounds
> to this remotest hilltop in Jamaica.

When she is finished she accepts a glass of rum from the engineer, thanks both men "in the grave high rhythms of the Victorians," and disappears. At that moment Birney becomes conscious of the fact that while she was singing he had simultaneously been hearing some Hit Parade western music from the porch outside; the engineer's steno and her boyfriend are crouched anxiously over a small transistor radio, oblivious to their own cultural heritage being paraded inside the cabin but eager to reach out for this offering of northamerican culture. He supposes "...they'd been listening to him / as exclusively as I to her / and out of just as much need / to exchange our pasts."

"Transistor" is an important and beautiful poem and Birney has given it a place of major significance in *Near False Creek Mouth.* Yet, although "Transistor" is the first poem in the first subsection of the book, it is in fact the second poem in the book as a whole. The place of honor in *Near False Creek Mouth,* in a place by itself, goes to the ominous "November Walk Near False Creek Mouth," which therefore seems to limit, define, and set the tone for the book as a whole. Considering Birney's belief in the necessity for the power of love and reason to come to the aid of a brainsick world, the lines from "November Walk" which refer to there being "More ones than twos on the beaches today / ...stranded as nations / ... / seldom the lovers   seldom as reason" are particularly significant, as are the allusions to an apocalyptic finish for the earth. It is as though, after attempting to create a unified view of Canada in his early works, Birney recognized that this would probably lead to expressions of narrow provincialism or brutish imperialism of the type he had parodied years before in "Anglosaxon Street":

> Here is a ghetto   gotten for goyim,
> O with care denuded   of nigger and kike.
> No coonsmell rankles,   reeks only cellarrot,
> Attar of carexhaust,   catcorpse and cooking grease.
> Imperial hearts   heave in this haven.

He went abroad for experiences that would help show Canadians that they were not *sui generis* but part of mankind as a whole. What he seems to have found, and is trying to express in this book, is that men are bastards everywhere. One can be mugged on the docks of Trinidad as easily as in New York City; the poor are everywhere and everywhere oppressed, especially by their own countrymen;

northamericans are ignorant, condescending, and imperialistic whether one meets them in Cuzco or on the Oregon coast; intellectual pretentiousness can be found as easily in a London pub as in a Canadian university common room.

Despite the increasing evidence of pessimism and despair which it manifests, *Near False Creek Mouth* is once again redeemed by Birney's constant sense of irony and his own genuine desire to reach out to people. The Trinidadian mugger at least has a quick wit; the randy poet suggests with a goatish wink just what it is that he intends to ask the beautiful girl who offers him a lift in her sports car; the naturalist's eye can still look past squalor and cruelty to the wild profusion of flowers that are the real "Caribbean Kingdoms." And, in one major poem, at least, Birney does stumble upon something which symbolizes his belief in the unity of mankind and in the need to bridge the gap between man and man. In "Cartagena de Indias" he goes wandering through a nightmare city where every tradition has been bastardized, where every human eye regards him with hatred, envy, or fear, where poverty and cruelty oppress him at every turn:

> city like any city
> full of the stench of human indignity
> and disarray of the human proportion
> full of the noisy always poor
> and the precocious dying
> stinking with fear   the stale of ignorance,

and suddenly he comes upon a pair of gigantic old shoes made of concrete and bearing an inscription that reads,

> In homage to the memory of
> LUIS LOPEZ
> we erect this monument
> to his old shoes
> the 10th day of February, 1957
>   [my translation]

Birney finds a bookseller who shows him a volume of Lopez's verse and explains that although Lopez spent a lifetime reviling his countrymen, in the end he said one nice thing about them: that they inspired in him "...that love a man has for his old shoes...." Hence the monument.

In a flash, Birney's despair and loneliness have been transformed:

> Descendants of pirates   grandees
> galleyslaves and cannibals
> I love the whole starved cheating
> poetry-reading lot of you   most of all
> for throwing me the shoes of deadman Luis
> to walk me back into your brotherhood.

"Cartagena de Indias" can be contrasted with the youthful Birney's "David" in the sense that here one finds practically the whole gamut of an older Birney's preoccupations expended on the same motif — the process of learning and communicating with humanity. The poem sums up Birney's rage at social inequities, his humor, irony, sense of history, certainty as to the importance of the poet's function. Moreover, it ends on a note of reconciliation and possibly a sense of absolution for his awareness of mankind's guilt, where "David" ended on a note of lost innocence. In "David" one regrets the death of the handsome youth, but the poem's solution to human problems is a kind of fascist toughness, where in "Cartagena de Indias" the solutions are humor, compassion, and endurance to the point where one can walk back into the brotherhood of man. This poem by itself goes far in making one agree with Al Purdy's opinion that *Near False Creek Mouth* contains the poetry of Birney's maturity, and that it is also the first book of his in which the presence of the author, formerly so well concealed, is fully apparent. Although the poems lack the intense dramatic and tragic quality of the earlier works, they are much more personal and humane.[56]

III *Years of Freedom: 1965–*

At about the same time that *Near False Creek Mouth* appeared Birney was preparing to quit the academic world in which he had labored, with time out for a war, for the last forty years. An indication of his discouragement with university life had cropped up as far back as 1955 when he had observed that creative-writing courses, which he had struggled so hard to establish at the University of British Columbia, were now "a cliché for university calendars, another enigmatic tag in the windows of our academic depart-

ment stores."[57] This remark was undoubtedly caused by his overall
sense of futility in the 1950s, but *Near False Creek Mouth* did also
contain poems like "Candidate's prayer before Master's Oral," a
relatively mild satire on the pedantry and the hidebound nature of
the traditional English Literature program:

> Now in my swollen suit of courses
> leaded round with dates and sources
> I bubble down   while memory swirls
> to fumble for the ages' pearls
> . . . .
> Guard me from blackout in the gulf
> and from the abysmal Beowulf
> Now may my Shakespeare hold at bay
> the Miracle and Mystery Play.

It also contained "Testimony of a Canadian educational leader," a
rather more stinging indictment of academic politics. The title is
particularly significant since the speaker, a thoroughly loathsome
but easily recognizable type, is offering his experience as a proven
formula for success, not as a *mea culpa*. He has risen by trimming
and by keeping his eye on the main chance:

> . . . just as my Satanic colleagues had it fixed
> with the Admin. to cast me out from here—
> my God is good—the Prexy's plane went down,
> and I was quickest to the New Man's ear.
>
> A Dean has duties too, but also Deanlets.
> One weekend I was Acting President.
> And were another plane to crash, and certain things
> told certain Regents—no, I'd not be hesitant.

These poems foreshadowed Birney's retirement from full-time
teaching in 1965. For the next three years he accepted appointments
as writer-in-residence at various universities in Canada and the
United States and then gave it up entirely. His experience as a
writer-in-residence was apparently neither stimulating nor particularly encouraging, as later poems like "1984 minus 17 & counting at
u of waterloo" were to suggest, and, "making him Writer in Residence for the University of Toronto may have blocked the idea conduit he has become from one generation to another. Few Professors
visit him. The ones that do make sure that their colleagues do not

find out. It is only the inquisitive, the adventurous young searching for answers to partially formulated questions, the intense students and the high school dropouts living in Yorkville that visit him."[58]

Fortunately for Birney, these inquisitive and irreverent young people, in whose company he has always rejoiced, did visit him and did stimulate him to become once again a "conduit from one generation to another." A quarter of a century earlier A. J. M. Smith could say that "...the new poetry is neither untraditional nor formless. Most Canadians have yet to get used to verse that has freed itself from the fetish of the exalted subject and the romantic cliche...,"[59] while at about the same time Northrop Frye had observed that "...culture seems to flourish best in national units, which implies that the empire is too big and the [colony] too small for major literature."[60] Frye had thus perhaps foretold the reason for the great outpouring of Canadian literature in the 1960s and 1970s, just as Smith foresaw what would have to happen before a poet like Birney could move into forms of verse that would allow him to express his true nature. The colonial position to which Frye referred in the same article as being "a frostbite at the roots of the Canadian imagination" had to give way to the sense of nationhood that emerged in the 1960s and that produced a general activism and freedom among Canadian writers. The influence of the Black Mountain poets like Duncan, Creeley, and Olson, the emergence of Op art and Pop art, and possibly the joyous sense of nationhood which resulted from the experiences of the centennial year, to say nothing of the youth movements of the 1960s in all their various forms, seem to have been the stimuli that Birney needed to break out of the doldrums of traditional form and to experiment with concrete poetry, found verse and poems pasted on mobiles or left loose in a binder to be shuffled at the reader's whim, even though his themes and preoccupations, within these new forms, remained the same as they had always been: social activism, protest at economic inequity, concern for natural resources, and, occasionally, a recurring poignant romanticism.

Before these influences appeared, for better or for worse, in his work, however, and while he was still shaking the dust of academe from his shoes Birney continued to write, edit, and publish his own work and that of other poets whom he esteemed. The major product of this period is his *Selected Poems* (1966). This large work gathered together once again many poems that had been out of print for some time. Some of them had been revised on points of fact — the hawks referred to in "David" are not kites — and many had been changed in keeping with Birney's evolving concepts of typography, punctuation, and layout; most of the formal punctuation was eliminated and the poems were laid out with special consideration for visual effect upon the reader.[61]

The critical reception of *Selected Poems* was mixed. While most reviewers were glad to have easy access to a large gathering of Birney's work once again, one critic pointed out that some of the poems were nothing more than self-indulgent reminiscences of personal experiences with little or no larger significance, and that the inclusion of these subjective bits of frivolity tended to weaken the book as a whole.[62] A. J. M. Smith in a very laudatory review observed that the last section of *Selected Poems,* entitled "Letter to a Conceivable Great-Grandson," is weakened by liberal propagandizing against the threat of nuclear destruction and the political problems facing the world in the period of the Cold War.[63] It is true that many of Birney's most pessimistic poems are reproduced in *Selected Poems;* "Remarks for the Part of Death" from *Now Is Time* reappears here as "Remarks Decoded from Outer Space," "The Ballad of Mr. Chubb" is updated from the *Trial of a City* version to incorporate the newly developed threat from Chinese nuclear weapons, and "Letter to a Possible Great-Grandson" from *Strait of Anian* has had its title modified to "Letter to a Conceivable Great-Grandson" and its contents altered to include the concept of horrifying genetic mutations which could result from a nuclear war.

On the other hand, in *Collected Poems* the radio play *Trial of a City* reappears adapted as a stage version under the title *The Damnation of Vancouver,* and in this case the alterations add both wit and polish to the occasionally sophomoric original. Captain Vancouver no longer is obliged to utter his cool judgments in jingling Gilbert and Sullivan rhyme, the reader is not condescendingly advised that William Langland wrote *Piers Plowman,* dates of birth and death for the historical characters have been added to provide a sense of realism and historical perspective, and a series of useful stage directions permit the reader to visualize the action as it would take place on stage. The character of Gassy Jack Deighton has been greatly rounded out; he becomes a thoroughly recognizable English working-class adventurer complete with West of England accent, a shrewd, cheerful rogue still lusting after the breasts and bottoms that cold death has forced from his grasp.

Despite the fact that a good part of the Salish Chief's lines have regrettably been cut back to make space for the new developments, *The Damnation of Vancouver* is ultimately much superior to *Trial of a City*. The new Gassy Jack is funny and memorable, and the play as a whole is much more balanced in its presentation of the various speakers; the stage directions add a professional touch and the play as a whole is less chastely "C.B.C." as a result of some added touches of sex interest, and Mrs. Anyone is more pensive, less chirpily optimistic, and therefore more striking than she had been in her previous avatar.

Finally, the poems grouped in the "Canada: Case History" section of *Selected Poems* follow Birney's familiar path from Halifax to the Strait of Georgia, but this particular grouping produces in the reader a curious sense of the emptiness and boredom of Canadian life. Starting off with a new version of the mocking "Canada: Case History" which updates Birney's long-standing doubts about the reasons for Canada's continued existence, its images evoke a raped and diseased Gaspé, a wearying transcontinental air trip, the life-destroying ennui of urban existence where the only worthwhile reality exists in dreams, the Laurentian shield empty of man and myth, the prairies vast and intimidating both in winter and in summer, and the shattered remnants of what was once a beautiful Pacific rain forest. One has an overwhelming sensation of a lonely, raddled land inhabited by human beings all too conscious of the facts of solitude and death. The *memento mori* motif permeates even cryptic love poems like "From the Hazel Bough" and "Haiku for a Young Waitress"; David's disastrous end at the hands of an unforgiving nature is paralleled by the self-destructiveness of the human mind in "Bushed." "Climbers" exposes one to a world of natural beauty and then reminds one that he must return to squalor, noise, and futility, and "Biography" relentlessly traces the path of man's physical decay. The whole group of poems is framed by the stoic acknowledgment of man's insignificance expressed in "Atlantic Door" and "Pacific Door." Even the liveliness of "Quebec May" and the brawling excitement of "Takkakaw Falls" cannot overcome the sense of forlornness and decay that underlies the invitation in "Gulf of Georgia" to

> Dive from the shining fluted land
>   through the water's mesh
> to the crab's dark flower and the starfish

> Trail the laggard fins of your flesh
> in the world's lost home
> and wash your mind of its landness.

Taken as a whole, these poems paint a portrait of a country that is cold, forbidding, and, worst of all, boring, and whose inhabitants, with old minds in young bodies, are locked in some barren nightmare.

Selected Poems is thus remarkable in that it reveals Birney's ability to pour old wine into a new bottle and produce a completely original effect upon the reader. It also set Birney in "a Janus stance," retrospective at the same time that he was considering new departures.[64] The new directions that his poetry was to follow did not really become clear until the publication of *rag & bone shop* in 1971, but in the interim there was plenty of evidence to show that he was as active as ever. In 1968 he published *The Poems of Earle Birney,* an inexpensive paperback which made available to his readers thirty-seven of his most important poems. In the same year he was awarded the Canada Council medal ". . . for distinguished achievement over an extended period, as a salute to a career of such duration that its nature has been unmistakably defined, and its merit and service to Canada has become evident."[65] From about 1959 he had been laboring, often under intense difficulties, to edit the works of his former neighbor, Malcolm Lowry; in 1962 he managed to publish *Selected Poems of Malcolm Lowry* and in 1968 he brought out *Lunar Caustic* by Malcolm Lowry with some collaboration from the poet's widow. In 1968 and 1969 he made a reading tour of Australia and New Zealand, and in 1970 he had the satisfaction of writing the foreword to *Acknowledgment to Life,* a collection of the poetry of Bertram Warr, a fine young Canadian poet whose work had first been anthologized by Birney in *Twentieth Century Canadian Verse* and who had been tragically destroyed by the war.

Among these fairly routine indications of poetic activity there could be found something of the new voice with which Birney was to speak in the 1970s. For one thing, his language had become raunchier as Canada's puritanical shackles slowly rusted away. Poems like "Way to the West" (1965), which refers to an atmosphere the color of "horseshit ochre" and to a "phallic Calvary / ejaculating essence of rotted semen" prefigured the explicit language that was to characterize his work in the years to come.

Secondly, there was the matter of form. As early as 1957 Birney had been calling for collaboration between Canadian poets and painters "to achieve that unity of figure and design and colour and word which can turn a book into a higher entity. . . ." Now, in the mid-1960s, he came under the influence of young poets like bp nichol and Andy Suknaski, who helped and encouraged him to develop these ideas. One of the results was *pnomes, jukollages and other stunzas* (1969), an envelope full of loose sheets and folders upon which are printed various "found poems," concrete poems, and more or less conventional poems like "Tea at My Shetland Aunt's" or "For Maister Geffrey." One poem, "Like an Eddy," is printed with each word on a separate piece of a mobile that could be cut out and hung up. There is a computer poem, "Space Conquest," a Joycean calendar "Pnome" for 1970, a handwritten version of "like an eddy" in the shape of an eddy, and some poems suitable for framing. "Alaska Passage" is printed one word or line per page in a brochure similar to a travel folder.

Clearly Birney was heavily involved in the concepts of nonlinear, unrestricted verse combined with new word forms. In some cases the experiment had valuable results; in others the results were less successful. Birney's early "Appeal to a Lady with a Diaper" neatly evoked the jouncing bus ride he had had to endure while listening to the prejudices of an ignorant boor; "Campus Theatre Steps" is a similarly happy marriage of theme and form. The "Pnome" calendar is funny and endlessly intriguing as it invites the reader to play with new combinations of dates and words, and the form of "Alaska Passage" brings the landscape of the North Pacific coast to the reader's mind more vividly than could the words by themselves. On the other hand, the habit of playing with words: "cancow" for "Canada Council," "anybuddy" ("any *buddy*") for "anybody," and the devotion to poems distorted into the physical shapes of the things with which they dealt became obtrusive. What started out as an experiment in poetic freedom threatened to trap the poet while it alienated the reader. Birney fortunately realized this in time to bring it under control before he published his next book of verse.

When *rag & bone shop* did appear in 1971 it marked a new epoch in the development of Birney's verse. Although it contained some poems ostensibly composed as far back as 1945, for the most part it consisted of fresh and surprisingly youthful work. The rather gloomy title with its gloomy origin is offset by the number of "fun" poems: "Pnome," "Window Seat," "Museum of Man," and many others that tend to laugh, however wryly, at man's foolishness and the poet's consciousness of his own aging. It also contains "For Maister Jeffrey," composed in 1959 and seeming to adumbrate Birney's turning away from the formalism of his early years toward the new, easy freedom in life and art that was to characterize him after he quit teaching. Lines like

> In Chauceres haselwood wher Robeyn pleyde
> Wher wren remembreth that the phenix seyde
> Wher Janus breeth blowth myrrh on misteltine
> I walken wol til al hys joy be myne.
>
> . . . .
>
> In Chauceres haselwood I walke alweye
> And never thynke out of his shawes to streye

can be seen as prefiguring Birney's renunciation of academe and his adoption of the permanent role of poet. Most striking of all, *rag & bone shop* contains many more spcntaneous and sincere love poems than did any of his previous books. Birney's love poetry, previously so rare and so cryptic, is here in surprising abundance and candor.

For all that, the book also reiterates some standard Birney themes. Canada is still boring, bourgeois, and ugly. Halifax is a mangy bear as "ugly as ever— / . . . with your paws at the end of rails / and your ass a port shitting for the world's wars." The students at Waterloo University are robots moving in brainless lockstep into the technocracy of the future. Winnipeg on a Sunday evening is evoked in a few vivid lines that call up memories of wind, dust, boredom, and puritanical mediocrity. There are some sarcastic prods at academic and bureaucratic pomposity, and a few humorous exploitations of the less flattering aspects of Canadian history and literature. But the poems devoted to these themes are far outweighed by those devoted to the two new and central themes that dominate this volume: Birney's consciousness of his own aging and the new freedom of his love poems.

The book opens with "once high upon a hill." The poem is an evocation of Birney's days as a youthful teaching assistant at Berkeley, but it ends on a note of regret for time past:

Was it like that at all?   or cant you hear me
& this is all a letter to the dead?   You don't remember?
No matter   whatever was   our ferris wheel went round
with gusto   its motion made a tune   a living one
allegro   not death's   his rigadoon wont sound
till all turning stops   & we are neither sideways
up nor blissful down   but free   for all   or nothing.

"The mammoth corridors" takes the motif of man's fleeting existence even farther back as Birney contemplates the efforts of the first native tribes to move down the interior of British Columbia and find a path to the coast, a movement which he relates to the westward movement of the white man, including his own parents, and which he recognizes as being ephemeral. When man's petty struggles and conquests are done the polar ice cap, "the Greenland lodger" who now lies "hoarding her cold passion" will return to establish "the rounded silence / a long hard peace." The poet's sad contemplation of his accomplishments is reflected in a poem translated from Oscar Oliva, and in "Four Feet Between" Birney struggles, as he always has done, to communicate with another man, only in this case the common element that he shares with a giant Fijian is that they are both sixty-five years old. He amuses himself with the thought of a spectacular suicide in "Window Seat," fights back to an approximation of his old randy self in "museum of man," and closes the volume with a "song for sunsets":

> goodnight big dad
> hasta la vista
> hasta luego
> we'll switch on now
> our own small stars
> lie in darkness burning
> turning
> through unspace untime
> & upsadaisy back
> i trust to you.

But if Birney devotes an appreciable proportion of the book to his awareness of time fleeting he does not do so in any morbid or defeatist manner. Instead, much of this surprising volume is devoted to a series of poems about love. The hitherto circumspect poet deals ruefully with the tenuousness of the marriage bond and

the brevity of human love; he longs openly for an absent lover in
"if you were here" and in a translation of Endre Ady's "if only
someone else would come," and exults like a springing youth discovering the joy and fulfillment of love in "i think you are a whole
city":

> ...yesterday when i first touched
> you i started moving
> thru one of your suburbs
> where all the gardens are fresh
> with faces of you
> flowering up

as he does in his manuscript version of "like an eddy." The two
motifs, a sense of age and an unabashed romanticism, are combined in the subtle "there are delicacies":

> there are delicacies in you
> like the hearts of watches
> . . . .
>
> i need your help
> to contrive keys
> there is so little time....

Thus, *rag & bone shop,* with valediction implicit in its title, turns
out in fact to be the introduction to a whole new and surprising
epoch in Birney's poetry.

Birney's next volume of poetry, *what's so big about GREEN?*
(1973), however, did not continue the dominant trends of *rag &
bone shop.* Instead of being introspective and romantic it turned
out to be Birney's fiercest and most despairing book. The twenty-
six poems include nature chants, concrete poems, a brilliant tonal
poem reproducing the sounds of a trip on a British train, a narrative poem, and even a love poem, but the greatest majority are
harsh denunciations of mankind's warmongering, mutual distrust,
and destruction of the environment. The overall effect of this volume is to recall a remark made by Northrop Frye in 1942 that Birney's realization that mankind is a temporary, unnecessary, and
even unsavory factor in the large pattern of natural history results
in a "tragic nihilism."[66] To a certain extent this nihilism has always
been characteristic of Birney's work, even when it was counterbal-

anced by some expressions of optimism or pushed into the background by Birney's experiments with new poetic forms, but here it absolutely sets the tone for the entire book.

The first poem, "daybreak on lake opal: high rockies," is a chant to the rising sun as the sun peeps over the mountain barriers and strikes the valleys, the peaks, and the lake with unimaginable beauty; but the serene glory of this scene only serves to accentuate the bitter satire of the next poem, "what's so big about GREEN?" in which Birney carefully analyzes the rape of the same lake. What was once a place of stillness and beauty and even a center of healing since there were sulphur springs nearby is now a raddled monstrosity:

> It was our fathers damned Opal
> bit out rock & gravel pits
> blasted off the stumps
> & hammered up a resort town
> Real progress for sure
> though no one believed my generation
> would be smart enough to finish it
>
> But we were
> ...kids buzz the lakelength
> in an hour of speed (on Speed)
> drag-racing round the stumps
> in the yellow waters
> No worry about hitting fishermen
> the last mercuric trout
> washed bellyupwards long ago
> & theres nothing that pullulates
> but algae & whatever bugs
> live on oil & shit

From this point the poem becomes a chant of hate and despair to more than counterbalance the chant of awe, devotion, and respect with which the book opens.

Moreover, the tone of nihilism is sustained as a sort of contrapuntal theme throughout the book: "i accuse us" details Canada's hypocritical but profitable participation in the Vietnam slaughter; "underkill" points out the rank inadequacies of the frontier gunmen who only shot each other one at a time; in "men's sportswear dept" even the plaster dummies would shrink from the touch of man if they could, "cucarachas in fiji" reminds us that we do not even have the staying power of this low form of life; and "the 21st century belongs to the moon" recalls once again the lines from "what's so big about GREEN?":

> Bare lava's best
> and cousin to the Sun
> That's where life is   genuine life:
> fire and atoms being born
> What's happened here on earth
> is only science fiction
> a nightmare soonest over
> Somebody had to get us back
> in step with all the other planets.

In the midst of this book of poems hymning man's savagery and folly, one comes upon some curious, poignant lines in "the shapers: Vancouver" which are reminiscent of those spoken by the Salish Chief in *Trial of a City:*

> with saw of flame
> vice of thong
> jade axe
> the first builders contrived their truce
> with sea and hill
>
> . . . .
>
> out of human fear & joy
> came the Shapes beyond lust
> the Fin totemic
> the incomputible rhythms
> the song beyond need
>
> . . . .
>
> we are lost for a way
> for a line
> bent for the mere eye's pleasure
> a form beyond need.

Reading this in the context of the book as a whole one is tempted to think that Birney himself is yearning back not just to his own youth but to a time before "civilization," before the white man, before Christianity. Such a point of view helps to explain the theme and tone of the two poems which open and close the book: "sunrise on lake opal" is a devout, sun-worshiping pagan hymn while "GOD" is a shapome made to look like a nondescript mutt and the title of the poem may or may not represent a heap of dog feces in the foreground.

Still, age, cynicism, and ill health have not managed to slow Birney down. At various times over the years he has suffered disease, broken bones, ulcers, severe eye strain, car crashes, a heart attack, and a severed sciatic nerve. Despite this he keeps traveling, writing, giving readings, and publishing. In 1973 a British publisher brought out *The Bear on the Delhi Road,* a selection of his previously published work; 1975 saw the republication of *Turvey* in an unexpurgated form as well as a two-volume *Collected Poems.* This last is a handsome and useful work, albeit sadly marred by the absence of some of Birney's very best poems. For reasons of space the editors had to leave out *The Damnation of Vancouver,* as well as "Joe Harris," perhaps Birney's finest war poem. They also left out "On a Diary" and "Moon Down Elphinstone," a fine ballad, previously uncollected. Birney compensated for these last two deficiencies by publishing them in 1976 in a slim book of poems, *The Rugging and the Moving Times,* a book which also contained "Interview with Vancouver," a continuation of his love-hate relationship with that city. But the real merit of *The Rugging and the Moving Times* lies in the restructured "On a Diary," in the beautiful and poignant "Moon Down Elphinstone," and in a collection of six love lyrics. These last, delicate and witty, serene and vigorous, tender and funny, are the continuation and refinement of the lyrical stream of love poetry which appeared for the first time in *rag & bone shop.*

Not long after Birney's first appearance as a poet A. J. M. Smith observed that Birney's generation as a whole had stopped exporting maple sugar and started importing new ideas and political movements as well as the poetic techniques of other nations in the twentieth century. They had become aware of the desperate necessity "to feel the tragic emotion and the sense of duty as a purifying and poetic force, not only upon a national but upon a cosmopolitan level...."[67] In this sense and in others Birney has long been a poet of the world, as the far-flung settings of his later poems would suggest. It is as though having "written the chronicle of modern Canada"[68] he then set about writing the chronicle of the modern world, a sort of literary anthropologist searching out and dragging home experiences of the great world in an increasingly despairing attempt to show men that they really are farthest neighbors. The

tone of his work may occasionally be despairing; it certainly is
nearly always ironic, but taken as a whole it represents an *oeuvre*
embodying themes, attitudes, and poetic techniques that merit
more detailed and specialized consideration in the following
chapters.

CHAPTER 2

Satire and the Comic Spirit

I Origins and Objects

WHEN Birney was working toward his first degree at the University of British Columbia in 1926 his graduating essay was on "Chaucer's Irony," a topic he was to pursue throughout his years of graduate study and which was to become the subject of his doctoral thesis. It has been suggested that Birney's habit of portraying himself in his own poetry, usually to ironic effect, is a habit that he acquired from his study of Chaucer.[1] There is probably no accounting for the ironic cast of mind itself; it is undoubtedly something that the individual is born with or else acquires through such a variety of influences that it would be futile to attempt to trace them to their sources. It is enough to say, as Desmond Pacey noted,[2] that Birney's characteristic stance has always been that of the observer, that this stance tends to make him isolated from or aloof to the scene observed, and that his typical reaction to much of what he sees is ironic or sardonic. Yet it may be possible to trace some parallels between Chaucer's background and Birney's: Chaucer was a member of the emerging middle class whose life was spent in the service of the ruling class; Birney was a member of the working class who spent his life in the service of the academic community. The common factor in each case is that the individual has been raised through a combination of luck and intelligence to a status above that into which he was born, and in each case the individual's intellectual superiority would tend to make him contemptuous of the class he served. Contempt openly expressed only makes enemies; hidden under a mask of humor it manifests itself as satire.

In Birney's case it was a good deal less dangerous than it had been for Chaucer to express his dismay at the world around him, and one therefore finds in Birney's work much more openly expressed criticism, more direct condemnation of folly than one does in Chaucer. Still, for the most part Birney manages to remember that a direct attack is less effective than one sweetened with a little humor, and he remembers too that he is as fallible and as prone to ridicule as the rest of the human race.

Birney's satiric vision illuminates nearly everything with which he comes in contact, from the billboard cluttered highways of Oregon to the stuffy Victorianism of Christchurch, New Zealand. He can sum up the essence of Christchurch — its work ethic, its social narrowness, its sense of history that seems to have stopped with Scott's death — by conceding to a local elderly reporter that yes, probably the luxury of wearing sideburns has been sapping Birney's intellectual vigor. The poem "Billboards Build Freedom of Choice" becomes all the more biting when one realizes that the Oregon coastal highway is one of Birney's favorite roads because of its great natural beauty. However, even though Birney is commenting upon the disfigurement of the landscape for commercial ends, the poem is principally a political satire upon the state of mind engendered in a nation whose thinking is dominated by slogans. Every statement in the monologue is nothing more than a slogan capable of being blazoned on a billboard; the speaker is delighted that "yedoan hafta choose no more," that everything has been made beautifully simple for him: "*two* parties is *Okay*," three means communism or possibly neutrality "like all dose damfool niggers in / in Asia somewheres...." What is more, aside from providing a handy source of predigested political opinions, the billboards also serve a utilitarian purpose. They give the motorist something to look at when there are clouds on Mount Rainier, they keep "de windoffa ya from allose clammy / beaches," and instead of anything so mundane as real cows they provide gigantic blowups of the ideal Borden's cow.

One of Birney's very earliest poems on any topic is "Mammorial Stunzas for Aimée Simple McFarcin," a withering attack upon the greed and fakery of religious fanatics and upon the simplemindedness of their followers. The evangelist herself is "soddenly ... gone with cupidities," her "bag blue sheikel-getting eyes" have disappeared along with the "dolourbills" that her credulous adherents had pinned to the wires strung across the inside of the tent where her revival meetings were held. If her disappearance leaves behind it an odor of greed and dishonesty, her victims, like those of

Chaucer's Pardoner, probably get what they deserve in the end. They are a "whoopaluyah mongrelation" who deserve to be made to pay for the cheap emotional thrills administered by their "mamomma" who is now permanently "lost from all hallow Hollowood O."

The goggle-eyed followers of Aimée Semple MacPherson only illustrate one aspect of man's pettiness; they believe that MacPherson's tawdry spectacle and her ability to rouse their emotions put them in some way in the presence of God; by pinning their dollar bills to the wires in her meeting tent they feel that they are paying off a debt which they owe to God for their sins. At the other end of the spectrum from this emotional bubble-bath one finds the point of view satirized in "Plaza de la Inquisición." The speaker protests angrily because he has found a dead spider in his coffee cup; "the waiter . . . [says] passionately nothing." The setting of the poem is all-important; after all the real passion and drama that have taken place in the Plaza de la Inquisición, the masses of people who have died there violently because of their views on man and eternity, a dead spider is merely ludicrous — or a dead man, for that matter. The waiter's passionate shrug reminds the speaker of his own relative insignificance: "It might be years / before I slipped and drowned / in somebody else's cup."

This same awareness of man's puny insignificance in the cosmic order is also fundamental to a whole series of poems spanning Birney's career. It occurs in "Remarks for the Part of Death" (1945), in *Trial of a City* (1952), and in "the mammoth corridors" (1971). The brevity of man's tenure on earth contrasted with his swaggering pretensions is a theme to delight the heart of Swift or Gibbon; Birney handles it in a poem like *Trial of a City* by having the dispassionate geologist calmly remind Legion that man appeared on earth fairly recently and probably, in geological time, has not much longer to last. In "the mammoth corridors" Birney reflects that all his frenetic activity, his mundane worries, his search for a little bit of his own past is as nothing compared to the past embodied in "that madcap virgin mother of ice / who embraced it all a wink ago in the world's eye" and who waits with infinite patience to "embrace" it all again. "Answers to a Grade-School Biology Test" and "cucarachas in fiji" make much the same point; man is in many ways inferior to the most despised of vermin; it is only his colossal pride that makes him ludicrous. And, as Birney reminds us in "Ellesmereland I," nature has no intention of

making the same mistake twice; she will not recreate man once he
has destroyed himself.

Another favorite target of Birney's satire is the squalor and misery resulting from social injustice. In "Late Afternoon in Manzanillo," for example, everything is reduced to the level of pettiness
and insignificance by the corruption of what could be a prosperous
society. The poem is filled with allusions to great religious and
mythical heroes, but here they are all rendered paltry by the setting
in which society has placed them. The two doctors who are frolick-
ing in the surf while they could be serving the diseased villagers are
named Lucas and Faustino. The classical Faustus traded his soul
for all the classical delights; this one is happy with a surfboard. The
carpenter, Jesusito, is

> hammering
>   with somewhat malarial
>   languor
>   a shrimpboat
>   to the ribshapes
>   of the galleons
> Cortez launched toward the Philippines.

The local shrimpboat captain is named Jason, but his golden fleece
consists only of some gold braid and his quest is for a prostitute
named Maria who sits in the Lane of Roses. The reduction of
heroic and divine figures for satiric social commentary is devastating.

Birney applies the same technique in "Hot Springs," his commentary upon the efforts of men to rejuvenate their waning sexual
powers. Here too he invokes the names of Montezuma and Diaz as
he observes modern men in their quest for eternal youth. The businessmen, bankers, and retired generals have access both to the
exclusive warm springs that are supposed to activate "THE
GLANDULAR / SEXUAL SYSTEM / BOTH MALE AND
FEMALE" and to the young prostitutes who roll up in expensive
Italian sports cars "to render / supplementary thermal assistance."
These worn-out men are searching for renewed sexual powers;
across the street by a cantina some dusty goatherds, like the priapic
satyrs of mythology, are "casually stripping / the ladies with their
fiery old eyes." The businessmen are searching for what the goatherds have; the goatherds are lusting for what the businessmen
have access to and cannot use.

But lying at the very heart of Birney's satiric vision is a contempt for anything that smacks of jingoism, racism, or nationalism, especially if it is Canadian. This particular aversion manifested itself in one of his very first poems, "Anglosaxon Street," and endured and developed over the years to include such offenses as Canadian anti-Semitism, the British Columbia centennial, New Zealand and Australian smugness, and northamerican boosterism in general.

"Anglosaxon Street" was written in reaction to the overblown patriotism of the early war years. The poem, Birney's most brilliant effort at recreating Anglo-Saxon alliterative verse, employs the heroic verse form and the kennings suited to events of the stature of the battle of Maldon or Beowulf's struggle with the forces of darkness, but into this heroic tapestry are woven the most petty and sordid details of a day in the life of contemporary urban slumdwellers. Instead of the magnificent beer-hall of the ancients there is the local beer parlor; in place of traditional loyalty of thane to lord there is the tawdriest of patriotism, engendered by wartime propagandists and expressed in slogans: "There'll Always Be an England" and "V for Victory." The noble queens who move with grace and dignity through the ancient poems are here represented by "farded flatarched / bigthewed Saxonwives   stepping over butt-rivers / waddling back wienerladen." The valorous thanes of old become today's ditchdiggers; instead of deeds of glory they dream of cracking the skulls "of nigger and kike."

Every aspect of the noble tradition is here debased, but the satire is not directed against modern working men merely because they happen to be manual laborers. Birney has plenty of sympathy for the people whose lives are reduced to a weary routine by the pointless rhythm of modern life, as his poem "The Ebb Begins from Dream" amply reveals. What he is satirizing in "Anglosaxon Street" is the organization of modern society itself, that urban society which robs man of the dignity of knowing why he lives and toils, that takes away the ancient myths and replaces them with B movies and patriotic slogans, that strips man of loyalty to his fellow man and turns him into a racist bigot.

This same spiritual sterility born of smug bourgeois assurance about one's own society and beliefs is parodied as well in poems like "Advice to a Hamilton (Ont.) Lady About to Travel Again" and "Most of a Dialogue in Cuzco." The Hamilton (Ont.) lady really need not bother leaving the tour ship to visit smelly, noisy Barranquilla. After all, as Birney sardonically points out, it may take a few millennia and a major shift in climate patterns of the globe but if she just stays on board the nice hygienic ship and goes home she will one day see Indians walking the streets of Hamilton in ponchos, peddlers selling spider monkeys on the streetcorners and boys hawking fresh-caught sharks in the Safeway store while passing taxis toot a few bars of Strauss. Why bother with the dirt and heat of Barranquilla? After all, cities are the same everywhere.

As for out-and-out racism, Birney dealt with that in "Restricted Area." As a general rule, he tends to attribute imaginary virtues to the non-Anglo-Saxon races; his French Canadians in *Turvey* are heroic, literate protectors of the weak, his Caribbean blacks possess great qualities of humor, tolerance, and brotherhood, his American Indians are invariably wise, noble, and generous in their speech and actions. Despite all this, Birney did have a legitimate target for his satire on the anti-Semitism practiced at some Ontario beaches. "Restricted Area" was written after Birney saw a "Gentiles Only" sign on a Lake Huron beach, and he claims that it was helpful in having racist signs outlawed in Ontario.[3] Intervening years have rendered the poem dated but in its time it was a potent example of the force of Birney's satirical pen.

Another object of Birney's ironic observations is the tendency for mankind to destroy its own past as it scrabbles for wealth. In "Conducted Ritual: San Juan de Ulúa" he presents an intricate satire of man's gutting and dismemberment initially of his own people, then of another race, and finally of his own history. On the island of San Juan de Ulúa in the Gulf of Mexico the Aztecs at one time conducted ritual sacrifices to their various gods; the sacrifice in these cases consisted of virgins who had their chests split open and the still-palpitating heart extracted and offered to the gods. Cortés turned the island into a prison for his Aztec detainees and, later, pirates and Americans fought over it at different times. Now the ironies of history are complete. The warring Aztecs and conquistadores are united in their descendants; those descendants are engaged in extracting money, the lifeblood of the nation, from tourists, mostly Americans, as official guides of the Tourist Office. What they offer the tourists is a potted and therefore gutted version of Aztec customs and the history of the island.

Birney is doing something similar in "what's so big about GREEN?", his lengthy, detailed chronicle of the progressive destruction of Lake Opal, a lake high in the Canadian Rockies containing a sulfur spring and long used by the Indians as a source of healing water. The first intruders were explorers and trappers who did little damage but who were followed by gold seekers, railroad builders, and finally the entrepreneurs who built the spas and tourist hotels. Now the rock paintings made by the Indians are gone, the salmon are dead, trees and flowers are destroyed, the water polluted. Birney's fury bubbles very near the surface, but its most effective expression is in the subtle way he capitalizes the pronouns referring to the white men who wrought this destruction, and in the fact that the last two words of the poem, "Our kids," are set in green ink. Green is the color of hope; "our kids" should have been our hope for the future but, if one takes the destruction of Lake Opal as a microcosmic example of what man has in store for the earth as a whole, there is not going to be a future for anybody, so "what's so big about GREEN?"

Finally, there is the matter of political enthusiasts. *Down the Long Table* is a serious novel about the Depression in Canada, the pitfalls inherent in human relationships, and the necessity for belief and action based on rational thought, but it is also a satire on the follies of young men who are led into dangerous adventures by their sex drives or by half-digested political doctrines. Gordon Saunders haring off across Canada on a freight car with two ham sandwiches in his pocket to "organize" Vancouver for the Communist party would be the ultimate in comic spectacles were it not for the fact that Saunders becomes involved, however innocently, in at least one killing and very nearly jeopardizes his future into the bargain. The book is crammed with satiric renderings of political jargon: a demonstrator who fought back against the police as they attempted to break up a rally in Queen's Park was "trying to grab the limelight for his uh counter-revolutionary fraction by uh — by ultra-leftist putschism."[4] Most of all, the book is a cautionary tale for young men who confuse their libido with their ideals. Gordon Saunders is so entranced by the luscious Thelma that he manages to convince himself that her selfish, indolent, ignorant family "were ... alive with intelligence and vigorous with purpose." Her gigantic harridan of a mother appears:

A veritable Earth Mother ..., saying little, but what she said folkwise, gentle, practical. Even the fact that she made no pretensions to grammar was, in the mood of the evening, a charming proof of her authenticity.[5]

Only later, when he is jilted by Thelma and in terrible personal danger, does Saunders realize the extent of his folly. *Down the Long Table* may be a chronicle of much of Birney's own youthful political idealism, but at least he has the grace ruefully to acknowledge that many of his postures were ludicrous.

Birney's ironic vision, then, takes in the entire scope of his experience from the time when he was a red-hot revolutionary youth to the time when age and weariness at man's endless folly push his satire very close to fury. The targets of his sardonic comments are anyone, of any race, whose pretensions or actions deserve to be held up to ridicule. In this, he does not forget himself; when he sits in judgment on the human race he remembers that he too is just one more human being.

II   Turvey

Although the ironic point of view with its underlying element of laughter is endemic in Birney's work, *Turvey* is far and away his best venture into comedy; it may possibly be the funniest novel ever written by a Canadian. It is an episodic novel relating the adventures of Thomas Leadbeater Turvey, a young man of limited education who had drifted about Canada from job to job until the outbreak of World War II. He then goes to Toronto to try to join the same infantry regiment, the Kootenay Highlanders, in which his friend Mac has enlisted. At every turn his attempts to join the Kootenay Highlanders are frustrated and his persistent attempt to win through to his goal provides the basic continuity in the novel.

Turvey is accepted into the Canadian Army, but not necessarily into the Kootenays, and does his basic training at Camp Borden. He later is sent to guard the Welland Canal; the tedium of this duty causes him to go AWOL to Buffalo, where he spends an orgiastic Christmas holiday before surrendering to the military police. After serving his punishment he is sent overseas to a replacement depot and while on a leave in London he stumbles upon Mac. The two are parted by circumstance and reunited on various occasions; during this time Turvey undergoes various training courses and gets himself into a variety of scrapes. Eventually he is sent to the Continent and blissfully becomes Mac's driver since Mac has now been commissioned. An illness separates Turvey from Mac once more and Turvey spends a time in various menial tasks before once more being allowed to follow the Kootenays up into Belgium. At Nijmegen he finally catches up with the regiment only to find that Mac

has just been killed. Turvey collapses and is found to have diphtheria; the remainder of the book is about his skirmishes with the
medical bureaucracy in England and Canada as he tries to free himself from the army and be reunited with Peggy, a British girl whom
he hopes to marry.

Since the novel is loosely episodic in form and since the background of each episode is only sketched in with sufficient detail to
give some sense of place, a greal deal of *Turvey*'s success depends
upon characterization. The character of Turvey remains an enigma
throughout the book; for example, the reader is never absolutely
certain whether Turvey is an idiot or merely an ordinary man of
limited education. Birney loaned Turvey many of his own experiences and many details from his own life. Turvey has the same
birthday as Birney; they both come from roughly the same region
in Canada; both worked at a wide variety of jobs before joining the
army; like Birney, Turvey tries to join the infantry and also like Birney he is invalided home as a result of catching diphtheria. But Turvey is Birney's alter ego in more than these superficial details; he
also shares Birney's great ability for making friends, his love of
travel, his suspicion of any bureaucracy, his appeal to women, and,
ultimately, his profound sense of the waste and tragedy of the war.

Apart from his resemblances to his creator, Turvey is something
of a Canadian Everyman. He is the figure who stalks through Birney's work — Joe Harris, the man on the tractor, the Indians on
the Delhi road — driven by economic and political circumstances
and yet searching for the things in life that all men want: love and
friendship, order, and stability. Within the scope of the novel his
immediate goal is simply to be reunited with his friend, but at every
turn larger issues impinge upon his search. Like every man living in
a modern society he must struggle to free himself from bureaucratic
controls, to keep society from placing him in a single restrictive
category, to find a means to breathe and develop in keeping with
the dictates of his own character. One can see in him something of
the reason for Birney's admiration for the great explorers; like
Bering and Cook and Drake and Hiram Bingham he must steer his
own course as best he may around the barriers that nature or
society place in the way of his questing spirit. In order to achieve all
this he must be tough, resilient, good-natured, and above all
endowed with the saving grace of common sense.

If Turvey shares some of Birney's own characteristics and background, so do the various Selection of Personnel Officers who pop

up from time to time to bedevil Turvey. The first is a dyspeptic former instructor in English at the University of Toronto. He is keenly aware of his noncombatant status and of his own lack of real medical or psychiatric training, and of what he fancies to be his intellectual superiority to the medical officers, corporals, and sergeants with whom he is obliged to work. Despite orders to the contrary he illuminates his assessments of the soldiers with Freudian and Jungian insights, which must later be deleted, and he manages to transform a rather simple case like Turvey's into something which, if his observations were acted upon, would engross the attentions of the entire psychiatric staff of the Canadian Army. At the war's end he is still in Toronto, divorced and a bigger nervous wreck than ever, but still trying to score a major success in the field of psychoanalysis. Turvey's last encounter with the Canadian Army takes the form of an interview he has with Captain Smith and from which Turvey emerges triumphant while Smith is left prostrate. Smith is the antithesis of Turvey; he represents intellect developed at the expense of common sense, he prefers theory to fact, and most of all he is quite out of touch with the lives of ordinary people.

It is the accurate delineation of the characters of ordinary people that enlivens the novel and makes it so accessible to the reader. Of these people, however, Mac turns out to be the least credible. His sporadic appearances in the book illustrate the fact that Birney threw him into the story as an afterthought to counterbalance Turvey's own tendency to resemble Sancho Panza. Mac is a success at everything he undertakes: he manages to join the Kootenays at the outbreak of war, goes overseas, appears in London togged out like a British gentleman, has an attractive girl friend with a flat of her own, and becomes an officer. None of these things is incredible by itself, but taken together they give the impression that the character of Mac was hastily tacked together to fill an empty space in the plot. Then, too, there is the fact that no Canadian ever spoke as Mac does. He is, after all, apparently a man like Turvey of limited education and yet he expresses himself in a curious telegraphic British, as tedious as it is unlikely:

Ah, poor boy. Letter may never reach me. Bad news. Didn't have heart to write it. Regiment came unstuck in Halifax. Broken up. Never found why. Not enough sober officers to take us over, expect. Cant wear badge even unless you're officer. See one of em occasionally. Scattered around. Odds and sods. No-fair-holdin units. Take a dim view of them. Expect you're in one now, eh? Number Twenty? Right. Languished there myself once. Posted now, thank God! Okanagan Rangers. Weird lot. Colonel's moustaches second-longest, Allied Armies, barring Ghurkhas. NCO's all farmers. No discipline. I'm one myself. Intelligence Corporal.

The best that can be said for Mac is that with his appearances and disappearances, his constant flitting ahead just out of Turvey's reach, he represents a suitably graillike object for Turvey's quest.

The characters of Turvey's peers are much more successfully drawn; in fact they are one of the great glories of the novel in that they form a composite portrait of the Canadian Army in wartime. There are the shy farm boys like Eric and Emil, lonely and disoriented in the crowded barracks and longing for their Icelandic community on Lake Winnipeg. There is Calvin Busby, the representative of the Alberta Bible Belt. There is Clarence, the medical orderly, fat, good-natured and gullible, the psychotic Ballard, a former juvenile delinquent who contributes to Turvey's going AWOL, and the alcoholic paymaster who defends Turvey at his court-martial. Then there are the professional soldiers, most of whom joined the army because they were out of work during the Depression and who now are either frightened or resentful at the prospect of having to go to a real war, and the officers, good and bad, whom Turvey encounters on his journey through the war. There is the black-marketing adjutant of the Pioneer Battalion at Poperloo, growing wealthy in the midst of starvation and misery, and the kindly major of the Medical Corps who befriends Turvey when he is most wretched.

Finally, there are the women who add a vital dimension to the novel in that their presence serves to remind the reader that this is not so much a novel about warfare as it is about human beings caught up in a war. For the most part, the women are working class, Turvey's female counterparts. They are lusty, good-natured, and unimaginative, but full of compassion, affection, and common sense. One of them will occasionally strike a sour note as in the case of the gold-digging Corporal Estelle who nearly succeeds in bankrupting Turvey on his first London leave, or the condescending British nurse's aide who cannot believe that Canadians are eligible for the Victoria Cross, but more often they are like the two jolly defense workers from Buffalo, who, working in shifts, keep Turvey supplied with sex and liquor during a much-needed respite from the defense of the Welland Canal, or like Turvey's fiancée, Peggy, who embodies all the anxiety, bravery, and self-sacrifice suffered by women in wartime.

One of *Turvey's* great virtues is that it combines low comedy with a form of high comedy that is at the very least a social commentary and which often verges on tragedy. The low comic elements are the foundation of the novel, the element which keeps the reader laughing and sustains his interest. They begin with Turvey's initial skirmish with Selection of Personnel Officers in Toronto and his first exposure to IQ tests. The tests and the Personnel Officers continue to be a blight on Turvey's existence throughout the novel; every time he gets into some scrape he is tested and interviewed anew. In the end, though, he emerges triumphant. By the end of the war he has seen the test so often that he scores 202 out of a possible 218 and sets ex-Captain Smith's heart aflutter in the belief that he has found a genius hiding in the body of a very ordinary Canadian working man.

Birney also uses *Turvey* to pillory the tedium and moronic addiction to routine orders of the noncombatant army. Early in Turvey's career, a misunderstood order sends him and thirty other recruits crashing over a condemned assault course with the result that Turvey gets a broken ankle and two weeks in the hospital. The boredom of guarding the Welland Canal inspires one of Turvey's comrades to use his fellow soldiers for target practice, and much of Turvey's time in England is spent on pointless courses, which he fails, or in the most menial of tasks; he even stays on in one camp as a doorman after he fails his officer training test. In Belgium he machine-guns his own greatcoat and one of the gateposts of the headquarters he is supposed to be guarding, and he and Mac drink everything they can lay their hands on.

But the true essence of *Turvey's* low comedy derives from what one critic complained of as Birney's "Rabelaisian reliance on the bodily functions and the Army's treatment of them which makes [*Turvey*] in many parts a very unamusing affair."[6] The critic undoubtedly had in mind Turvey's marathon love-fest with the two defense workers, or the scene where he accidentally washes his genitals with permanganate, or his encounter with stereosphagoscopy in a Belgian hospital, or the manner in which he organizes a cozy love nest for himself and some friends with the help of some female Belgian collaborators. However shocked Canadian critics may have been by these earthy adventures when the book first appeared, those same adventures have proved to be one of its most enduring attractions. Their truthful and bawdy humor has made Canadians laugh for two generations.

Turvey's lustful inclinations lead him into an attachment to Peggy, his British fiancée, and his efforts first of all to see her, then to ask her to marry him and finally to get back to her from Canada where the army has discharged him provide a lighthearted counterpoint to his continuing and ultimately tragic search for Mac and the Kootenay Highlanders. His efforts to rejoin Peggy are the stuff of music-hall comedy; in these scenes Turvey is the eternal fall-guy driven by love and lust toward the object of his heart's desire and forever doing pratfalls just when victory is in his grasp. Each time he seems on the verge of being reunited with the buxom Peggy he runs afoul of army regulations, is posted away from her, confined to a hospital bed, or sent home to be discharged. Love-struck youth has ever been the subject of light comedy, and Turvey in all his fumbling sincerity is a classic example of the type.

Much of the reason for *Turvey's* enduring appeal to Canadians of all ages must derive from the fact that in addition to its earthy low comedy it also contains a stinging commentary on warfare; it is also a comedy so high that it approaches tragedy. Turvey's resemblances to Schweik or Sancho Panza are fairly evident, even if they are somewhat superficial. He shares with Schweik and Panza, and Huckleberry Finn, for that matter, the common fund of good sense and level-headedness that brings the ordinary man through a scrape where the idealist or the romantic visionary would probably be destroyed attempting to pursue his fantasies. Like Schweik and Panza he goes where he is sent, in the course of someone else's war, without complaining and without ever questioning the forces that generated the war or demanded that he play a part in it; if anything, he is eager to serve: "I got my call-up so I come here to go Active and be a Kooteny Highlander, please sir." And like Schweik or Panza he endures an infinite amount of being shunted about aimlessly in the great but imperceptible pattern of the war.

Once these resemblances have been noted, however, the comparison must cease, for in fact Turvey is no simple-minded Schweik moving unthinkingly on the path of least resistance, just as he is no crotchety old Sancho Panza grumbling at the heels of a man he considers to be insane. Turvey's ideals are high and serious; he is shocked to learn that the Regular Force Corporal Boggs with whom he guards the English coastline has no desire whatever to engage in combat: "I joined for a good place to sleep n'eat thout having to

work m'ass off. That was in 37. Dint figger on no war then." For
Turvey, aside from the occasional lapse into dalliance with the local
women and liberated spirits, the war is a very serious business; he
and Mac have come a long way to do their part and he entertains no
doubts, at least at the start, about the importance and rightness of
their task.

It is this sense of innocence and idealism established early in the
novel that intensifies Turvey's and the reader's disillusionment as
the war and the novel progress. Turvey's frustration at the boredom of the training camps in England and at his inability to get into
action are genuine and justified. When he does get over to Belgium
and sees the black-marketeering Canadian soldiers in action he is
deeply shocked. Even in this safe rear echelon the grimness of his
surroundings begins to impinge upon his consciousness:

There was already a sullen glow over the flat white land in the east when
the highway at last funnelled between lombards frosted like bleached fish-
bones, and narrowed into the town of Poperloo. They passed ragged old
men plodding topcoatless in sabots on their way to the morning Winter-
Help queue, and a single labourer in patched green corduroys clutching a
dinner pail.[7]

And as Turvey finally achieves his goal of going forward to the
theater of action where he will be reunited with Mac he "wasn't
nearly as happy as he thought he would be. It wasnt that he was
scared.... Perhaps it was the chill January day and the bleak
sights along the highway."[8] The bitter weather, the dead civilians in
the Dutch town through which he passes, the old men and tired
women struggling to keep from starving or freezing; all of these
experiences serve to rob the war of its glamour.

At the end of his odyssey, after another brief delay while the
army decides once more whether or not to let him fight, he is
reunited with Mac. Coming as it does near the end of a comic novel
the shocking tragedy of the reunion spares the reader nothing of the
horror and disgust that Birney felt for the war. Turvey is ill with
diphtheria, Mac has been killed just before Turvey could reach
him, the whole scene is set in the bitter cold and darkness of a north
European nightfall. At this point there is nothing funny about Birney's comic novel, and he follows up the impact of Mac's death
with a continuing litany of the horrors of war. Turvey's further
adventures in England and Canada resume something of their former comic tone, but Turvey himself sees the world through wiser

and maturer eyes. Formerly robust, he is now debilitated, and on the way home he sees more of the wreckage of war: the young sergeant with no legs, the Flight Sergeant still dreaming of bailing out into the flak over Berlin, the boy with his jaw shot away, the bombardier with no testicles; this part of Turvey's journey is a journey into hell.

If anything, *Turvey* resembles *Catch-22* more than it does *The Good Soldier Schweik* or *Don Quixote*. There was nothing quixotic about Canada's participation in the war, as Frank Scott demonstrated as early as 1940; it was imperialistic, precipitate, and at that time unjustified.[9] The Canadian soldiers for the most part may have gone, as Birney himself did, with a sense of duty and high purpose but somewhere along the line, like Yossarian and Turvey, they must have lost their illusions. Turvey himself strongly resembles Orr in Heller's novel, a cheerful, simple man who toils away at being a soldier and who ultimately makes up his own mind about what the war means and to whom. In the end, Orr deliberately gets his bomber shot down in the Mediterranean, takes the tiny rubber survival raft with its spoon-sized paddle and paddles out of the war, all the way to Sweden. Turvey's ultimate victory over SPOs, the army, and the bureaucracy at large is very similar to Orr's. He relies upon his own common sense and what he has learned from Mac and his experiences in the army to fight free of the system. Orr frees himself by means of a diminutive paddle; Turvey uses his false teeth to terrify the bureaucrat who would enchain him once more, and he gallops out of the army into the blessed sunlight of freedom. *Turvey,* like *Catch-22,* is a funny novel with horror at its center.

III *The Comic Poems*

Of all the comic subjects in Birney's work, he himself is easily the one that recurs most often. The tendency to laugh at his own foibles is what helps to counterbalance his satiric comments upon the rest of the world. Sometimes, as in "Waterton Holiday," he is merely laughing at the ludicrous spectacle of his own body:

> I too shall spread myself anyhow,
> presenting these dry legs
> scraggly as a saskatoon bush
> to whatever comic Canadian bogle
> has arranged this trance.

But more characteristically his humor is tinged with sadness. "First Tree for Frost" is apparently a whimsical commentary upon his own childish ineptitude; his father planted a spruce for him, he was not satisfied with its rate of growth and tried to help it along by urinating on it, and it died. When the funny tale is ended, though, he wryly recognizes in his childhood mistakes a paradigm of his later life and concludes sadly that "some things my loving never has convinced." This combination of the satiric vision with sadness at the human condition also characterizes "On the Beach," in which the poet recognizes that he himself is now on the beach, an old hulk, and that he will only make himself ridiculous if he tries to match the speed and grace of the young girl running lithely along the sand.

Much of Birney's comic poetry depends upon the ridiculous aspirations and actions engendered by his own randy sexual desires. In "Twenty-third Flight" he takes a mocking look at the "wild hopes" entertained by "this one aging sheep" when he is met at the Oahu airport by a lovely hotel courier. The poem develops into a wry commentary on his own aging, and ends with an astonished bleat of injured vanity: can it be possible that the courier will pass Birney up and lead "another old ram in garlands" past him to celebrate the sacrifice of her virginity? The same prurient comedy enlivens "Curaçao" and "museum of man." In "Curaçao" he praises the courtesy and friendliness of the natives, but leeringly suggests that he is going to put that courtesy to the test when he asks a special question of the hotel clerk's lovely sister, and in "museum of man" we have to laugh at his adolescent delight in the chance to try on scores of twelve-inch penis sheaths.

Sometimes Birney's laughter results from the sudden relief from fear. "Meeting of Strangers" begins on an ominous note: Birney is alone at dusk on the Trinidad docks; he is surprised by a black mugger who creeps up behind him with a knife. Up to this point the danger is very real and the reader can sense it:

> there was a glitter
> under the downheld hand
> and something smoked from his eyes.

Then, as Birney prepares to fight for his life, he is saved by the sudden appearance of a taxi. The humor of the poem is heightened by the fact that the reader is made privy to a joke known only to Birney and the mugger. The taxi driver is left in the dark by the parting line, but Birney and the reader can laugh at the mugger's quick wit.

A whole series of Birney's poems derive their comedy from an Alice-in-Wonderland logic where everything abnormal is normal. The prime example of these poems is "Six-Sided Square: Actopan," which consists of a series of gnomic answers to the questions posed by a female tourist. A six-sided square is not normal, in fact it is technically not a square, but Birney insists that everything in Actopan is normal even though "patterns more complex must have precedence." He then proceeds to ring changes on the words "normal" and "mean": "Actopan is a town more average than mean" where one can see "a brace of ancients... / under separate sarapes in a common mescal dream," where the "ladies work at selling hexametric chili" while their "normal sons" bounce an oval (not a round) basketball about the square (which is a hexagon). Today is the feast of a "median saint" who rates a "medium celebration" and "hexametric" devotions. To understand all this the woman must realize that "Actopans are all rounded [squared] with the ordinary [the mean]."

"Six-Sided Square: Actopan" is one of Birney's ways of dealing with the intricacies of Mexican life. The local church is Christian, but it was built, like many Mexican churches, on the foundations of an Aztec temple; the worshipers pray in Spanish to the Christian saints but their instincts urge them to use an African dialect and to direct their exhortations to pagan gods. Ordinary logic is useless in a situation of this complexity, so the poet reverts to the sensible nonsense of Lewis Carroll and the verbal subtleties of James Joyce.

Joycean doubletalk is fundamental to the humor in *The Damnation of Vancouver* and Joycean wordplay is also combined with the tradition of nonsense to produce a whole series of "pnomes" and "colanders." The technique in all cases is the same as that employed in "Six-Sided Square: Actopan": Birney presents the reader with a situation taken from the "rational" world and then contrasts that situation with a nonsense version. Hence, Legion in *The Damnation of Vancouver* struggles vainly to establish a case based upon formal logic only to be ambushed at every turn by Powers's doubletalk: "Your question's once again misleading, Mr. Logion. Our method of bomb-nation's not yet subtled."

"Pnomes" according to Birney are "gnomic mnemonic pomes to remember things like the kooks of the monk and who wrode them." In fact they are calendars in which the names of the months have been scrambled to the point where they provide an amusing alternative to the usual names, but guarantee lunacy for any reader who tries to make an exact correlation. "Janissary" and "Marsh" do not vary greatly from "January" and "March," but is "Cassiwary" an equivalent of "February"? "Jubilee" suggests the glories of the month of June, but what is "Burn Off"? Birney helpfully provides footnote memoranda to names of past and succeeding months: "Marsh" was preceded by "abe" and will of course be followed by "rillway," just as every schoolchild knows that "Hog Toe" is preceded by "bernault" and followed by "femmebeure." The point, of course, is that laughter is not tied to any form of logic; in fact, the heartiest laughter can be a result of freeing oneself from logic's bonds.

Birney's world of illogic also involves fantasies about flying. He ponders man's inability to fly in "First Flight" and "Window Seat." The former is an account of his childhood attempt to fly by leaping off a barnyard gate. He had previously convinced himself that the feat could be accomplished if no one were watching, and after he crashes to the ground he realizes that his attempt was sabotaged by the hogs peering at him through the slats in their pen. He realizes sadly that there will always be some kibitzer to spoil the fun but remains convinced that if he could live in a world totally to himself the rules of logic, like the law of gravity, could be suspended. The persistent irony of life that mocks the foolhardy pretensions of the intellectual is that he must exist in the presence of swinish proletarians whose down-to-earth observations prevent him from attaining the divine status to which he aspires. This same resentment of a meddling world is the subject of "Window Seat." Birney toys with the idea of setting new records for swan dives, gainers, and somersaults by diving off the wing of an airliner at 35,000 feet, but such nonsense is forbidden by a society that keeps a firm grip on its Turveys. The man who dreams of a godlike act must instead await a mundane ending to his life "somewhere / at ground level / under the overcast ahead."

Birney's fantasy poems shade off at times into whimsy, as in "Professor of Middle English Confronts Monster," "Tea at My Shetland Aunt's," and "cucarachas in fiji." Most of these poems are amusingly ironic reflections upon confrontations between man and the natural world. The "monster" encountered by the professor of Middle English is a harmless lizard in a Caribbean garden. Birney amuses himself by describing the beast in heraldic terminology and then deflates the image by comparing the lizard's puffing and deflating throat to a teenager chewing bubblegum; this humble comparison of course reflects upon Birney himself as a watered-down Saint George.

"Tea at My Shetland Aunt's" is based upon the same device. The poet sits musing among the mementos of his family, of distant countries visited, suggestions of an ancient literary tradition and strongly held religious beliefs, while the old lady rambles on about an encounter with some sparrows. Man in his picayune distractions is at his most comic. Another form of confrontation, this time between man and cockroach, occurs in "cucarachas in fiji." In this case there is nothing picayune about nature's representative; the cockroach turns out to be a formidable beast, having existed for 350 million years and still going strong, with 1,200 species in existence. There is every chance that they will outlast man on earth just as they long preceded him. Birney has some fun exaggerating the cockroach's taste for insecticide and Gideon Bibles; the insecticide is an aperitif to them but the religion will surely ruin their digestion. In this case, though, Birney's whimsy takes on some of the aspects of gallows humor; the inevitable conclusion is that man is less than a cockroach, except possibly for his ability to laugh.

Then there is the humor that Birney finds in the victory of the weak over the strong. Legion and Powers being routed by Mrs. Anyone lend a lighthearted comic touch to what would otherwise be a sanctimonious ending to *The Damnation of Vancouver;* the small boys of Barranquilla wreaking their "rough justice" upon the bigger boys, and the beldams of Tepotzlan deftly shortchanging the wealthy tourists clearly delight Birney's heart. One can see this same pattern of the human comedy in "giovanni caboto / john cabot" and "charité espérance et foi." Cabot exemplifies the hustler being hustled: he brings back some cod and a few bearskins to Henry VII and tells the king that he now owns "cipango   land of jewels / ... / also the spice lands of asia / & the country of the grand khan," whereupon the king gives Cabot thirty pounds and tells him to go back to Nova Scotia. Charité, Espérance, and Foi are three girls whom Champlain adopted and "civilized" in the hope of showing them off to the court of France, but when a merchant attempted to seduce them they threatened to cut his heart out and eat it, so Champlain regretfully had to cancel his *coup de théatre.*

There is a certain amount of truth in Birney's belief that Canada is practically devoid of comic literature. His poem "our forefathers

literary" suggests that only Haliburton and Leacock contributed
very much to Canadian humor; the rest were unutterably solemn
and straitlaced. This may have been because there was relatively
little to laugh at in the early years of Canada's development; pio-
neers struggling to survive in a wilderness usually encounter very
few comic situations. Later, of course, there were the great wars
and the Depression, none of which were humorous events. In the
last forty years, however, a comic note has crept into Canadian
writing. If the country still has not produced a Mark Twain or a
Laurence Sterne it at least has the wry and often bawdy observations of poets like Irving Layton, Al Purdy, and Birney himself.
Canadian humor, when it does appear, tends to be satirical perhaps
because the strongest impulse is to mock the puritanical mores that
dominated the country in its colonial beginnings, or possibly the
irony derives from the poets' awareness of man's Lilliputian size in
contrast to the grandeur of the country itself. Whatever the reason
may be, Canadian humor is characteristically ironic, and Birney is
therefore in the mainstream of what seems to be a new element in
Canadian literature.

CHAPTER 3

Love and Death

I *Introduction*

BIRNEY'S work is marked by an almost total absence of love poetry in the early years, and what he did write tends to be cryptic and anonymous. As Desmond Pacey observed in 1952, "[Birney] is not a very passionate poet."[1] This situation underwent a radical change some years later, but when Pacey made the statement it was certainly true. Part of the reason for the shortage of love poetry in Birney's early work may be found in Birney's own contention that young poets tend to be better at expressing hate than love;[2] Birney found plenty of things that aroused his wrath or contempt in his early years as a poet and these considerations may have distracted him from the writing of love poetry. Another critic noted that when Birney did write love poems they were ". . . elegiac and autumnal. . . , or, when not elegiac, at least about love at a distance (e.g., 'This Page My Pigeon' and, in a sense, 'The Road to Nijmegen')."[3]

One could add that in the 1940s Birney was handling the theme of friendship with much more assurance than the theme of love. Poems like "Within These Caverned Days" and "For Steve" display an openness and sureness of touch that is missing from the poems mentioned by Milton Wilson and also from other love poems like "St. Valentine Is Past" and "From a Hazel Bough" whose obscurity and ambiguity may be a deliberate attempt to conceal Birney's real attitude toward the relationships between men and women. For example, "David," Birney's magnum opus, deals squarely with the ultimate test of human friendship, not love. Certainly, he seems to have been cynical about the fickleness and even murderous characteristics of a certain type of woman. Lena in "The Ballad of Mr. Chubb" is a cold-blooded murderess, Comrade Kay in *Down the Long Table* is cruel and neurotic, Thelma in the same novel is empty-headed and selfish.

Birney's attitude toward women in general, then, was rather suspicious and stand-offish, as though he were never really at ease in their presence. Yet, they tend to dominate the male characters in his work. The father figures: Turvey's, Mr. Barstow in *Down the Long Table,* Joe Harris's, Mickey's in the short story "Mickey Was a Swell Guy," are elderly and shadowy; often they are ne'er-do-wells resembling Pap Finn who are either already dead or in the process of drinking themselves to death, leaving the stage clear for the powerful mother figures. Joe Harris cries out poignantly to his mother, perfunctorily to his bride, not at all to his father.

Part of the reason for Birney's failure to write much love poetry in his early years may also have been the fact that from childhood he seems to have been aware of the transience and uncertainty of love; the whimsical tone of "First Tree for Frost" only partly conceals his chagrin at the inevitable fact of death and at the difficulty of transmitting the quality of one's love to another creature. This same vein of sadness can be discovered everywhere in Birney's work: even a poem like "Aluroid," which could have been left as a humorous mock-heroic about a house cat vainly stalking wrens in the garden, is given a pessimistic twist in the last line. At this stage in his poetic development his awareness of the omnipresence of death, his doubts about the female character, and a certain innate reserve seem to have combined to inhibit his writing of love poems.

II *Early Reticence*

As late as 1962 Birney addressed a poem of friendship to George Lamming with the words "To you / I can risk words about this." In this case Birney was not restrained by timidity but by the thought of how difficult it is to express one's feelings in words and also by a natural reticence about openly displaying his emotions. If he was this reluctant to discuss his feelings about a friend in 1962 he was infinitely more circumspect in the love poems of the 1940s, where he consistently adopts a careful anonymity. He never specifically identifies the subject of his early love poems. To whom was Birney speaking in "Cadet Hospital"? Who is the woman with a voice as sweet as mead and with gentian eyes? Thirty years later he added the dedication "For Esther," but in its first appearance the identity of Birney's loved one was carefully hidden.

The same anonymity characterizes other contemporary love poems like "This Page My Pigeon" and "Invasion Spring." "This Page My Pigeon" may have been addressed to Birney's wife but there is no evidence to support this contention and the reader must be cautious about making any such suppositions. "Invasion Spring," for example, appeared without any dedication in *Now Is Time* but was reprinted in *Strait of Anian* with the words "For M.C." Similarly, "The Road to Nijmegen" had no dedication in *Now Is Time* but was dedicated to "Gabrielle" in *Strait of Anian*. These dedications were deleted from subsequent printings of both poems.

The care with which Birney conceals the identity of his loved ones is compounded in some cases by a cryptic style that occasionally threatens to obscure the meaning of the poetry. It is this quality which renders "St. Valentine Is Past" both intriguing and baffling. The poem is apparently a statement of Birney's inflexible belief that love is as transitory as life, but it may also be read as a cautionary tale for the timid in love. If Theseus and his pack represent certain inhibitions that have kept the lovers from consummating their passion, then when those inhibitions are temporarily forgotten the lovers find they have waited too long; time has either killed their love for each other or else has robbed them of the ability to perform the act. The second and third stanzas are full of fertility images: waterfalls, sunlight, a spring suddenly freed from a rock, and the gusts of passion that these images suggest momentarily override the restraints, the "jeering gullish wings / far crashings in the glade," that have hitherto kept the lovers in check.

The imagery of the fourth stanza suggests time wasted, sterility, and dormancy, but both this stanza and the one following promise that now the lovers will unite in love and procreation. No longer will one lover be a promise of fertility unfulfilled by the other, no longer will timidity prevent the man from uniting with his mistress. But all of this lush anticipation is squelched in the seventh stanza when the lovers come to realize that they have waited too long. Incapacity and boredom have robbed them of love both physical and spiritual; their bright hope of building "a dam of love / and [dappling] all the meadow" turns out to be only a pathetic promise of love that comes too late. By the time they are ready to consummate their love "Theseus with his pack," i.e., life with all its restless force, rushes upon them once again and they turn back into their timid selves like "huddled woodbirds." The poem is rich in the symbolism and imagery both of the life force and of sterility, but Birney's reticence conceals his full meaning from even the most careful reader.[4]

Birney's early attempts to deal with the love relationship tend also to be stilted where they are not cryptic, as though he found himself ill at ease when he moved away from his characteristically ironic detachment. Thus, in "This Page My Pigeon" he lapses into unfortunate lines about "the rightness of hills" and "the saneness of music and hemlocks," and in *Down the Long Table* the exchanges between Gordon Saunders and his mistress are especially mawkish:

He clutched her knees. "Anne, you're wrong, I do want children, my children. And I want you. It's not too late—"
She shook her head almost with pity. "My dear, if I went through with this, you would have to take me with three kids — perhaps none of them yours."
Say it, say you will anyway.
But how, when? I would never—

Later in the same novel when Saunders attains a certain objective viewpoint more in keeping with Birney's own, he is saved from such soulful lapses by an awareness of the potentially ridiculous nature of his attachments.

III   *The Transience of Love*

Running through Birney's love poems is the persistent awareness that human love is a very shortlived thing; *tempus et amor fugent,* and the awareness of this fact leads him to something very near despair. A poem like "From the Hazel Bough" may be full of images of life, beauty, and vigor, the lively meter may suggest the joy and freshness of youth, and the penultimate stanza may claim a jolly, flirtatious, cavalier attitude toward love:

> we winked when we met
>   and laughed when we parted
> never took time
>   to be brokenhearted

but the last stanza shifts abruptly to a sad reflection upon death and the loss of love; ever at the latter end of joy comes woe:

> but no man sees
>> where the trout lie now
> or what leans out
>> from the hazel bough.

Even in a cynical poem like "The Ballad of Mr. Chubb" there is a note of sadness. Chubb is a pathetic figure for all his failings and one cannot help feeling that perhaps once Lena did truly love him before she was tempted into betrayal and murder. The same note is sounded on a more serious level in "On a Diary":

> Love dies more often than the flesh,
> starves quietly in body's absence.
> . . . .
>
> How then to choose when the outgrown lover returns
> reproachful with wounds but deaf in his alien heart?

"Lament"[5] is another of Birney's early poems in which he expresses his doubts about the permanence of love. The loved one whom he addresses shares all the beauty of the stars and the blue mountain lake, the softness of a forest stream, but like the star, the breeze, or the stream, her beauty and their love are passing things that will shortly disappear. Birney often takes the wind as a symbol of the brevity of life and love, or to represent the chance meetings and chance partings of human beings. In "Wind Chimes in a Temple Ruin" the two glass leaves suggest the accidental coming together of two lovers under the impetus of a love that is as transitory as the breeze which first moves them and then passes on, leaving them still.

Birney's doubts about the permanence of love are intensified when he deals with the question of marriage. "The Marriage" is a sardonic commentary on the tendency for passion to ebb with time, and an observation on the fact that counteracting this tendency is more important, and more difficult, than finding food and shelter. After outlining an idyllic life for himself and his wife in the two opening stanzas, the poet ends the poem by saying,

> in time we'll find a way perhaps
> to use this driftwood
> to keep the tides
> from ebbing every day,

suggesting that the real problem for any married couple is to maintain interest in each other, to keep the tide of love from ebbing, and that all they have to work with is "driftwood," bits of flotsam picked up from various theories on how to maintain a happy marriage.

The restless, untamable sea is also used in "like an eddy" to suggest the shifting nature of love. Birney expanded the original two-line poem to ten lines and entitled it "still," a poem in which the original words of "like an eddy" are rearranged in various sequences to suggest the washing in and out of a tide about a rock, a tide which jumbles and confuses the order of things and undermines the assurance of the words in the first two lines: "like eddies my words turn / about your bright rock." The poem ends with a faded subscript repetition of the title, "still," as if to suggest that the poet's assurance in the calm, still, rocklike center of his love may be writ in sand.

"o what can i do" is a cryptically morose commentary on Birney's own marriage. In *rag & bone shop* it is the second of two poems written "for esther"; after the list of superlatives that Birney combines to form the initial letter of Esther's name in the first, concrete, poem, he shifts into a wry series of observations upon the inability of any two people to remain in exact harmony: "o how can i keep with my nipping old mare / & how can she wait for me?" This belief is one which reaches back to the beginnings of Birney's poems on love and marriage. He says that he originally conceived the poem "Mappemounde" as an ironic comment, in the style of Hardy, upon the transitory nature of love and faithfulness. He began it while he lay ill in an English hospital awaiting departure for Canada on the hospital ship *El Nil,* formerly the private yacht of the libertine King Farouk, when he overheard the promises of deathless love exchanged between Canadian soldiers and their British sweethearts. It occurred to him to wonder how many of these sweethearts and lovers would be waylaid by the "mermen" and "mermaids" of everyday routine and forget about each other completely.[6]

A somewhat sadder, less cynical version of the same idea is expressed in "Monody for a Century," written rather earlier than "Mappemounde." A monody is, after all, a lament sung by one person and thus is characteristic of Birney's sense of loneliness at the passing of love and the coming of the war. The title of his very fine poem "The Ebb Begins from Dream" also implies that from the high point of dream — either a sleeping dream or a waking dream or ideal of perfection in society, of happiness in life, of joy in one's work — one ebbs toward the reality of life with its grubby jobs, absence of love, squalid living conditions, fatigue, aging, and death. Whether Birney is regretful or wry or openly cynical on the subject of romantic love, as he is in "found swahili serenade," he is consistently preoccupied by its brief and often illusory nature.

One of the results of Birney's doubts about the durability of human love is the persistent note of loneliness in his work. It has been said of the dialogues in his poems that "... the conversations ... are metaphors for the essential loneliness of an articulate observer."[7] Birney himself was deeply interested in the work of Malcolm Lowry, and he once said that Lowry's poems formed "... a record of the intense inner world of a supersensitive, suffering modern man."[8] The motif of loneliness in Birney's work is clearly evident in poems like "adagio" and "the gray woods exploding," and it forms an essential element even in comic poems like "Twenty-third Flight"; Birney might joke about being passed over by the young courier but he is aware of the fact nonetheless.

In "adagio" the stranger approaching in the night at first appears to present a threat; he is a "great ghost." Then as he draws near he becomes Birney's equal, a fellow human being, a "familiar," in fact. Then as he goes on his way he inevitably shrinks and disappears, leaving Birney with his loneliness. The movement of the adagio is slow, but this only lends poignancy to the theme of lost friendship. This theme is compounded in the more intricate "the gray woods exploding." The basis of the poem is the story told by a young lecturer about a man, possibly himself, who has spent his life on the move, never remaining long enough in one place to form any deep attachments. He marries a woman whom he loves deeply and who helps him finish his studies. Just as they seem about to begin a settled domestic life, she dies of cancer and he is left to live on alone. As he finishes the story, Birney, in an attempt to reach out in sympathy, makes a tactless guess at the identity of the man in the story and the storyteller lashes out at Birney for his impudence and then retreats into his shell. The possibility for communion and friendship has been destroyed. One is almost tempted to believe that the lonely figure of the intelligent, sensitive, versatile university lecturer, so careful of his privacy, represents one of Birney's own alter egos; the poem with its multiple layers of loneliness may in some sense be "about" Birney himself.

More direct references to loneliness as the natural condition of
man and to the ineffectiveness of marriage as a cure for that condition can be seen in poems like "Tavern by the Hellespont," where
Birney, sitting alone, reflects upon the fact that even if Xenophon
or Leander or Byron were suddenly to emerge from the shadows of
history no real rapport could ever be established between them and
Birney despite the multiplicity of their interests; they would eventually find themselves as solitary as the two tourists sitting nearby
who are alone despite the fact that they are linked by marriage.
Even in a poem like "i think you are a whole city," with its tone of
joy produced by the discovery of a new lover, there is still a note of
uncertainty vis-à-vis the loved one. Birney is never completely sure
that his love is, or can be, reciprocated. The poem ends on a note of
solitude; Birney is back in his "single bed," only dreaming that he
has been allowed to enter the new city.

Yet, despite these uncertainties, in Birney's later work there is a
reaffirmation of his belief in the powers of love and affection. Even
when he says that "this increasingly creative world of ours is
increasingly conformist, negative and destruction-bent" he goes on
to say that as far as he can see the only countervailing forces are
love and art, even in the presence of death.[9] George Woodcock has
said of Birney's work that "one is aware all the time of an irritable
vitality, at times joyful but more often impatient, and impelling
that search for brotherhood, for the lost links between persons and
peoples that becomes, with the need for wandering which is its
other aspect, the great theme of Birney's later poems...."[10] This
last is certainly very true; Birney is fully aware that "love dies more
often than the flesh / Love starves quietly in absence," but he also
knows that human beings must go on loving if they are to survive
and that poets must go on expressing this vital truth.

IV   *New Influences*

Aside from Birney's personal inclination toward circumspection
when it came to expressing his love for another human being, there
were also social pressures that would tend to stifle such expressions.
Dorothy Livesay has commented upon Canadian poets' traditional
fear of being thought sentimental and upon their heritage, from the
British colonial period, of an attitude which forbade overt expressions of emotion.[11] Perhaps the tradition of the stiff upper lip may
have been as stultifying for Birney as were the Canadian censorship

laws; and this may help to account for the fact that in all of Birney's work there is no open suggestion of affection between father and son. He may have needed the Free Speech movement and the youth movements of the 1960s to help him give voice to what had been repressed during the "silent generation" of the 1950s. The lack of an audience which would have appreciated openly romantic or even erotic poetry would have been as stifling as the censorship laws regarding four-letter words.

What all this tended to produce in Birney's work was a valetudinarian note; repressed emotion and sexuality are transformed into a consciousness that life and time are passing. The *ubi sunt* motif of poems like "From the Hazel Bough" is one aspect of this effect; the warning about letting love and time slip by expressed in "St. Valentine Is Past" is another. The dominant theme of *Near False Creek Mouth,* taken as a whole, could be aging and death; the poems written about foreign places often include references to ancient societies like that of the Incas, ruined cities like Machu Picchu, elderly people and old places. The poet returns to Vancouver to walk by the seashore in the autumn before the coming of the winter's cold.[12]

This tone, of course, did not suddenly appear in Birney's work in the 1950s. He had written "David" when he was thirty-six years old, and he says, "I began to see that it was the passing of my youth I was mourning.... I felt a deep need, a compulsion, to express this inevitable change from carefree happiness, this loss that none escapes unless he die young."[13] And in "Biography," published in 1949, he had given voice to the idea that man begins by loving life and in the end is worn down by it. At ten or twenty, the man in "Biography" is undaunted by the "swords of snow," and if the lake is taken as a metaphor for his unknown future, a "bright unpredictable book," then the "rainbow" can be either trout or dreams of a glorious future. At this point, death is not for him: "Only the night-mists died at dawn," but by thirty he is "trudging" along and becoming more aware of "the peaks" of life's struggles and dangers; he has forebodings of old age when he sees "the veins of bald glaciers." By forty, time is already moving too fast for him; he is mastered by the weight of the years: "a shrill wind shouldered him / and he turned." In the end he forgets the lake of his youthful dreams, loses his nerve, and dies.

On the other hand, some of this world-weariness and sense of aging is offset by those lyrics of Birney's that suggest that love exists and can be of vital importance to humanity: poems like the speeches of Gassy Jack, the Salish Chief, and Mrs. Anyone in *Trial of a City*. In a poem like "Bangkok Boy" one sees Birney's belief that innocence and vitality are good and that they do exist, at least until they have been touched and corrupted by the world and time. And "A Walk in Kyoto," with its specifically sexual imagery — "a carp . . . rising golden and fighting / thrusting its . . . body up from the fist / of a small boy. . ." — used to resolve the frustrating and perplexing man / woman, male / female, native/foreigner oppositions that Birney has developed earlier in the poem, hints at the departure from traditional reserve that was increasingly to characterize Birney's work in the 1960s and 1970s.

There is such a strong tendency for Birney's heroes to die young — David, Joe Harris, the various explorers in his poems — that one is almost tempted to think that he is deliberately saving them from the fate of becoming middle aged and middle class of which he himself was so contemptuous. Yet, when he was well past middle age his work was marked by a sudden blossoming of love lyrics. It is almost as though Birney realized and fought back against the fact that his love reminded him of his own mortality. Gone are the stoic acceptance of youthful death, the sardonic commentaries, as in "Twenty-third Flight," upon his own failing powers as a seducer, the gloomy acknowledgment of the weight of time, as in "Biography." When Birney was nearly seventy he began to write a remarkable series of love poems in which lyricism replaced much of the previous sardonic note, which are marked by a totally uncharacteristic romanticism, and which are addressed, also in a manner quite untypical of Birney, to a specific individual.

One of the problems that Birney encountered as he grew older and which he resented very much was the restriction placed by society upon love among the aged, the paradox of love and sensuality continuing into old age and being faced with social strictures and taboos. Something of this problem is reflected in poems like "St. Valentine Is Past," where the aging lovers are sundered by the force of youthful nature, and in "Haiku for a Young Waitress." This last is a serious version of the ideas underlying "Twenty-third Flight": the loneliness of the aged is exacerbated by the fact that they are still capable of desire and are daily faced with desirable objects. The "dusk" of advancing years is rendered more poignant by the fact that an impenetrable "holly hedge" of social custom separates the poet from the youth and love of the young waitress, who is beautiful as the dogwood.

Faced as he was with effects of age, of passing time, and of social custom, it appears that Birney decided not to give in to these forces but to fight back to the very end. He had already acknowledged the evanescence of things in poems like "From the Hazel Bough" and of his own failing physical powers in other poems like "On the Beach," but now he came forward with a series of love lyrics that can only be called an act of defiance in the face of death. One of the earliest of these poems is "if you were here," written in 1970 and published in *rag & bone shop*. "if you were here" is one of Birney's very best love lyrics; it is less strained and more heartfelt than anything he had written before and it has a beautiful natural rhythm that seems to derive from the poet's serene contemplation of the fact of his love. It is true that the poem is marked by a mournful note:

> as from some soundless warp of time i watch
> but not with you—the great ships of oceans
> come swirling thru the sparkling pass below
> while over them at dusk the baldheads glide
> the tallest firtops sway in secret dance
> &—see!—sunset's firing ice along the Olympics!
> but you're not here to see....

The poet's joy in the beauties of the natural world is counterpointed by his reiterated longing for his absent wife; nature itself seems to lack a dimension because she is not there to see it, but, for all that, the poem remains a powerful statement of emotion most unlike Birney's usual ironic stance.

Except for "i think you are a whole city" there is nothing else in *rag & bone shop* to compare in tone or attitude to "if you were here," and in Birney's next volume, *what's so big about GREEN?*, there is nothing that can be called even vaguely romantic, with the possible exception of "there are delicacies" and the story told by the young professor in "the gray woods exploding." "the gray woods exploding," however, looks back to and owes its romanticism to the "sundered comrades" motif in "David" and *Turvey*. It even represents a reworking of "Joe Harris" since it takes the "Joe Harris" story and inverts it; the wife dies but the husband lives on. For all of these reasons, then, it is part of an earlier tradition in Birney's work and not part of his new romanticism.

The greatest outpouring of Birney's love poetry is to be found in

The Rugging and the Moving Times (1976). Here, his traditionally mocking tone toward women and love and toward his own entrapment by them is sublimated into a subtle blend of affection, spiritual union, and reconciliation with the fact of his own mortality. In "the miracle is the stream," for example, those natural elements, wind and waves, which had previously served to symbolize the transience of life and of love are used to symbolize the permanence of love and a calm acceptance of the fact of death. Age and youth are joined in an endless cycle of love that death cannot break:

> the magic is the wind that moves
> a lily's unfolding lips
> to lean in the dark
> & touch the face of a wrinkling lake....

The awareness of the imminence of death is fundamental to most of these poems. It underlies "the miracle is the stream" just as it does "On her twenty-sixth birthday" and "she is," but it is an awareness that stimulates the poet to new effort; death is a fact that he can accept because he is secure in his newfound love. As Birney says in "Omnibus," where he humorously portrays his lover as "a new city bus,"

> behind the clear round
> of her windows
> through a still possible world
> she carries me loving
> and safe in herself....

Some of Birney's old, wry humor can be seen glimmering in these poems, but the bitter edge of irony has been subdued; he can laugh at himself but he is content with his lot. He sees himself as a nervous old father grouse fussing around the nest and unable to settle down because the hen is away, or he is a hapless pedestrian who has to be borne safely away from danger by the "omnibus" powers of his lover. He may be some sort of a wild creature caged by the powers of the telephone, or a timid child appalled by the vastness of an empty bed. Regardless of how he sees himself, the self-mockery is gentle and, in the end, compensated for by the return of his lover or even by the fact of her existence. By extension, one could say that Birney's world-view was altered by his late-blooming love. The fierceness and despair that disfigured *what's so big about GREEN?* occur as well in some of the poems in *The Rugging and the Moving Times,* but they are at least counterbalanced if not totally nullified by the great beauty and gentleness of the love poems.

These poems also represent the drawing together of some strands that had been woven through Birney's poetry from the very beginning. In one of his earliest poems, "Flying Fish," death appears in the form of a dolphin, at once terrible and beautiful to the flying fish that it pursues, even as death must appear to human beings who accept it rationally. Then, in poems like "Bangkok Boy" and "The Bear on the Delhi Road," there is the element of pity at what the world does to its creatures. The bear wished "to stay / only an ambling bear / four-footed in berries" but forces beyond his control, the pressures of existence, in fact, destroyed that idyllic life forever. Both of these poems share the same sense of urgency engendered by the prospect of age and destruction; it is important to live as intensely and as long as one can, and at the same time to greet death almost as a friend when it comes. This idea and this attitude toward life and death come together with Birney's attitude toward love in a poem like "Ballad of Kootenay Brown," about a hell-raising remittance-man who wins the love and respect of his Indian wife through his gentleness and manliness. He predeceases her but returns, she thinks, in the form of an airplane that is forced down in the Waterton draw. She stumbles into the propeller and Brown in his new avatar "kisses her dead." There is neither irony nor mawkishness in the poem; it is a statement by Birney of how love and death can become reconciled, and how man can accept the fact of death if he knows that he lives on in the spirit of his loved ones.

CHAPTER 4

The Mythological Element

CONSIDERING Birney's early reading of the Old Testament, *Pilgrim's Progress,* and the lives of adventurers in distant lands, it is easy to understand his interest in mythology and the place he gives it in his own poetry. His reading of Old and Middle English for his graduate research, with the concomitant study of Norse and Germanic sagas, would only have helped to deepen and strengthen his interest in mythology. Paul West has commented upon Birney's "urge to myth," saying that Birney "has always been something of a animist. For him the temperate Canadian pastoral [keeps] leaping into pageantry, bestiary and something close to the heraldic."[1] In fact it is not just the temperate Canadian pastoral that is alive with mythological import for Birney; an experience like meeting two poor men driving a bear down the Delhi road or the discovery of what is to him an inexplicable metal stela in an Australian mining community triggers his myth-making fantasies. Birney is always creating a mythology of the future, as he does in "the 21st century belongs to the moon," just as he is always looking back to that of the past. The bear and the Australian stela are experiences that can only be accommodated by being transmuted into myth.

On the other hand, Birney has no belief in God; he has said as much[2] and one could infer this fact from his irreverent picture poem "GoD," which takes the form of a rather unappealing mutt. Birney makes much use of Judeo-Christian mythology, but his own religion seems to be based upon whatever goodness can be found in the human character; as he says to the Cuzco priest, "I . . . am not deceived / by your cold deity." Rather, Birney tends to be like the carpenter in "El Greco: Espolio" who ignores Christ standing behind him while he gets on with the task at hand. The carpenter's medium is wood, upon which he works with all his concentrated energy; Birney's medium is words and inherited myths, and he works upon them with the same fierce concentration. They are old material to be shaped into something new and better suited to the world in which Birney finds himself.

There are a surprising number of mythological references scattered throughout Birney's work, from the hint in *Turvey* that Emil the Icelander represents the Norse tree of life[3] to the more obvious and less successful references in "North Star West." At least the first quarter of this poem is greatly weakened by being crammed full of random allusions to mythological events. Stanza one refers to Noah's Ark, but stanza two jumbles up the Wooden Horse with the Amazons, while stanza three introduces Bellerophon's stallion, Pegasus, and stanza four hints at the Book of Psalms: "we lie like lambs in the lion of science" combined with references to the Persephone myth: the stewardess transforms the plane and its passengers into a garden of flowers "yet herself is deftest flower of all."

In "North Star West" Birney's insistent use of mythological allusions is intrusive and tiresome, but many of his other poems depend for their success upon the skill with which he manipulates the element of mythology and the way in which he recognizes myth as forming a necessary link between man, time, and nature. "The Bear on the Delhi Road" is an outstanding example of this technique. The origins of the poem are well known: on a trip into northern India in 1958 Birney saw two Kashmiri men driving a bear they had captured in the Himalayas down into the hot plains and cities where they would teach it to dance and thereby perhaps earn enough to stay alive.[4] Birney felt a link of common humanity between himself and the two Kashmiris and probably between the three of them and the bear as a representative of the natural world. All four of them were in some way bound together on a journey whose end they could not foresee and also by economic forces which they could scarcely understand and yet to which they had to respond for their very lives. How was the poet to express this sense of commonality and pity? First of all, he invokes the powers of myth to place men and bear in a new perspective; instead of being an ignorant brute driven along by human masters the bear becomes "unreal tall as myth" while the men "spindly as locusts" leap about him. The relationship is that of accolytes serving a deity.

Subsequent lines suggest that the bear shares some of the qualities of a classic hero entranced by some witch or siren; the accolytes do not wish to kill their servant/deity; they simply realize that it is essential to awaken him from "the tranced wish" to remain merely a beast. They must free him from the reality of being just an "ambling bear" in the berry patch and bring him to the point where he can assume mythic dimensions, i.e., the beast must become manlike and perform manlike acts. Since he comes from "the fabulous hills" he therefore must be able to achieve this fabulous transformation.

And yet, in the end, the power of myth and the external force of the real world are not subject to the whim of man. One spell gives way to another. The bear is to be freed from "the tranced wish" to remain a mere beast; he will assume some of the characteristics of a man, but ultimately he and the Kashmiris and Birney himself will find themselves trapped in another spell. They will all have to lurch together as best they may "in the tranced dancing of men." This is what Birney means when he says that "it is not easy to free / myth from reality"; the two are interwoven beyond the powers of man to disentangle them.

A rather more obvious instance of Birney's use of mythological references occurs in "November Walk Near False Creek Mouth." Milton Wilson was the first critic to note that the people whom Birney observes in the poem are updated figures from various religious and mythical traditions,[5] and Frank Davey performed most of the remaining task of running down the fabulous trails that Birney had laid throughout the poem. Some of the traditions referred to are the Greek: "the horn of Triton or Merman," *"Prince Apollo," "Princess Helen,"* "Mykean islands," "Gate of Lions"; the Hebrew: "a troller ... lies longdrowned / on an Arrarat of broken clamshells"; the Christian: a "wrinkled triad of tourists / ... / seeking a starred sign ... / dangle plastic totems   a kewpie / a Hong Kong puzzle for somebody's child / who waits to be worshipped / back on the prairie farm"; the Teutonic: "I'm one of the Lockeys! / ...the Lockeys of *Out*garden ... / ... / ... then you must know Carl Thorson?"; the Buddhist: "the gamey old gaffer / asleep on the bench like a local Buddha"; and the Canadian Indian: "where shamans never again will sound / with moon-snail conch the ritual plea / to brother salmon or vanished seal."[6]

Birney's use of mythological references in "David" is rather subtler than in "November Walk Near False Creek Mouth." Up to

Part VII of the poem, David and Bob are merely high-spirited boys enjoying their youth and strength in the open air of the Rockies. The talk is all of climbs successfully completed, of knowledge gained, of success, friendship, and peace, of hats full of raspberries, and peaceful sleep under the stars. Then, abruptly, in Part VII all these boyish things are left behind and a new note of high seriousness creeps in. David becomes the "chevalier sans peur et sans reproche" who has undertaken many adventures with his squire (Bob) but who must now go forth to dreadful and final battle with the Finger. As he passes, "the quiet heather flushed" like a maiden blushing for her warrior knight. David yodels at the mountain sheep and sends them fleeing as a brave knight would drive in the enemy's pickets and sound a defiant trumpet challenge to the enemy himself.

Then David and his squire "fight" their way up to the enemy's citadel. At the moment of victory David is treacherously defeated by his corrupt enemy; the "rotting tip" of the mountain gives way under his foot and, like an enchanted person, "without a gasp" he is gone. Bob later finds him stabbed in the back by "a cruel fang / of the ledge"; like a good squire he tends his wounded lord on the field of battle, but it is no use. David can hear the spinning wheel of the Fates in "the purr of the waterfall [rising] and [sinking] with the wind" and he knows his time is very near. Like Arthur ordering Sir Bors to fling Excalibur into the lake, he orders Bob to perform one last, unthinkable service, and like Sir Bors, Bob "[grasps] for a lie." Bob is full of the guilty knowledge that David was betrayed by the carelessness of his squire, who should have covered his back in the presence of the enemy.

Finally, David absolves Bob of his guilt and Bob performs the last service for his lord. This act will make of Bob a true and mature knight in his own turn, but first he must make a long journey of expiation; he must search "in the blackness" for the trail to self-knowledge and serenity while the dreadful beasts — "gaping greenthroated crevasses," "the fanged / And blinding seracs," the snouted glacier, "the humped moraine," and the "spectral larches" — menace him on every side.

This same technique of using mythological suggestion to lend additional dimensions to various poems can also be seen in such diverse poems as "Bushed," "Aluroid," and "Takkakaw Falls." In "Bushed" the trapper invades the ogre's territory, slays and eats its inhabitants, and uses parts of their bodies to decorate his clothes. Too late he realizes that the ogre has been watching him all along. The wild goats and the ospreys are lookouts and skirmishers; "the night smoke [rising] from the boil of the sunset" suggests the witches and sorcerers in league with the ogre; the moon, the owls, and the cedars threaten and mock him with mysterious totems and incantations, and the winds are busy forging the secret weapon that must destroy him.

All of "Takkakaw Falls" is a reworking of the myth of the dying and rising god. The river thunders from his own cloud like Jupiter or Thor, is hurled from his mountain fastness by superior forces, and his own subòrdinates help finish him off: "His own gale rends him" and he crashes, still magnificent as Woden or Zeus, to his death. But his last dying act is to "batter the brown throbbing thighs of his mountain" and miraculously he reappears, triumphantly reborn from the sea to grow slowly in strength and win his way back to his own kingdom.

In "Aluroid" Birney turns to the tradition of Bast, the Egyptian cat-deity. He transforms a small Siamese housecat into an awesome and mysterious figure. The wrens which she stalks are potential sacrifices to her fierce demonic power; ultimately they turn out to be defiant heretics, mocking her divinity as they flee.

Finally, there are those poems in which Birney comments upon the mythology, or its absence, in a given country. "North of Superior" and "Our forefathers literary" are cases where Birney is all too conscious of the lack of an indigenous Canadian mythology. The absence of such a tradition has hampered the development of Canadian literature inasmuch as it has deprived it of a dimension enjoyed by the literatures of other countries. Try as he may, Birney himself finds it impossible really to believe that the vast, barren Laurentian Shield can ever have been the home of troll or Scylding, witch or questing knight. It is merely barren rock, lakes, and scrubby fir trees, hardly the stuff of romance.

On the other hand, to Birney Mexico is a country possessing a mythology which it cannot escape. Mexico does not forget her history because she cannot. In "Six-sided Square: Actopan," despite the poem's persistent references to normalcy, the average, and the commonplace, the fact emerges, especially in the last stanza, that the Actopanos live and think according to ancient and unusual codes. Even as the speaker ironically insists that everything is normal, intrusive evidences of their real world impinge upon the speaker's awareness; the Actopanos are bound together by the

Ottomiac language, by "a common mescal dream," by whatever symbolism may reside in hexametric piles of chiles, and by their pre-Cortesian religion. The contrast between "North of Superior" and a poem like "Six-sided Square: Actopan" or "Pachucan Miners" seems to underlie Birney's attitude toward mythology and its uses; most countries have a usable mythological tradition which their poets interweave almost unconsciously into their work, but Canadian poets have no such tradition. If they want to add a fabulous dimension to their work they must borrow the fables from someone else and superimpose them on their own poems, and the resulting poetry is quite different in each case.

I   *The Uses of Mythology*

Birney uses mythology in his poetry for a variety of reasons: to add a dimension to the fact of the Canadian wilderness and its non-history; for satiric effect in contrasting the mundaneness of contemporary life with the heroic aspect of olden times; to relate modern-day events and experiences like World War II to archetypal experiences; and occasionally to project a mythology of the future.

"David" is an example of myth being used to add a dimension to what is on the surface at least a story of the Canadian wilderness. The heraldic connotations lift the poem to the plane of a quest story, a motif common enough in Birney's poetry; in fact, it is this motif that lends a tragic aspect to *Turvey*. In one sense, Turvey is not a comic picaro but a questing knight. Like so many of Birney's other heroes, including David and the professor in "the gray woods exploding," he learns about life through intense personal suffering; in Birney's poetry, only those who suffer actually learn, and they therefore are New World counterparts of the questing and suffering heroes of antiquity, including Beowulf and Percival.

Birney's use of mythological references to add meaning to essentially nonromantic and nonmysterious areas of industrial enterprise may also be seen in poems like "oil refinery," where the use of alliterative verse, and the equating of the oil to a dragon and its treasure hoard, and the refinery workers to warriors who must trap the dragon and steal its treasure, relate the struggle for existence of modern man to the struggles of classic adventurers.

At other times the references to myth and fable serve quite another purpose. It has been remarked that "North of Superior"

"...is filled with more or less erudite allusions to Scyldings, Excalibur, the Green Knight, the Den of Error, Azazel and Roland...."[7] The implication of this remark is that Birney tried unsuccessfully to see heroic traditions where none existed. Yet this is not the case; Birney has said that in " 'North of Superior' the interweaving of phrases from literary classics ... are deliberate interruptions...; they are asides to my own voice, to underline the contrast between the storied landscapes of Britain and the traditionless wild of the Laurentian Shield."[8] For Birney, mythology is important as evidence of human thought, creativity, and the power of the poetic imagination. Yet it is an element which he does not find in raw nature; the natural world by itself is beautiful but harsh and indifferent. This fact underlies one of the paradoxes of Birney's universe: he loves nature and is fully aware of its beauty, but in order to be fulfilled as a poet he requires myth, the fruit of the human brain, i.e., of creatures whom he detests as a group. Man may be the most destructive force in the world, but nature without man and his myths is empty, impersonal, lacking in a dimension.

Thus, in Birney's more successful poems one often finds classical mythology wedded to the Canadian wilderness. The success of "Takkakaw Falls" depends upon the attribution of godlike qualities to the river. The Promethean journey of the river, however, never overwhelms the nature imagery. Even though the poem opens with an invocation of Jupiter and Thor the poet is careful to sustain the reader's sense of mountain and gorge, of the essentially New World aspects of the scene. There are the persistent and subtle images of "upslant ledges," fir trees and cliff edges reaching up to the clouds in the first half of the poem, and in the second half the newborn-god imagery is neatly balanced by that of the lowland river scenery; the classic Old World story of the dying and rising god is interwoven with a sparkling picture of a wilderness river winding its way around boulders and silty bottom land to the sea. Moreover, there is something lighthearted in Birney's treatment of the classical element; the god falls, but not through the machinations of an enemy; the suggestion of disaster and suffering is softened by the constant references to sunlight and rainbows and by the vivid evocation of the beauties of the Canadian Rockies. The two elements, Old World mythology and New World natural beauty, are here combined with the happiest of effects as each permeates and renders the other more vivid.

Birney's use of classic allusions to add an often humorous

dimension to his nature poetry is also evident in a poem like "Aluroid" with its puns, its grotesque imposition of godhood upon a small house-cat, and the sudden seriousness of its ending. Bast was the Egyptian goddess who presided over childbirth; she was the personification of life and fruitfulness at the same time that she was a war goddess and protector of cities. To saddle a tame Siamese with all of these attributes is laughable, just as the contrast between the terrible preoccupations of a war goddess and the few wrens who are the cat's prey is ludicrous. When the cat hears her dish being filled in the kitchen she immediately turns back into a small domestic animal. These contrasts, along with the puns (the cat steadies her tail into "an Egyptian frieze"), lead the reader humorously along until the final line where Birney reminds us that the wrens are real and that they have escaped one death only to fall into another. Still, the overall tone of the poem is playful; Blake's tiger is consistently exotic, but Birney's aluroid is exotic only to the extent needed to point up a domestic irony.

Birney's comic use of myth, however, can shade rapidly into satiric social commentary in poems like "Late Afternoon in Manzanillo" or "a small port in the outer fijis." These poems depend for their ironic impact upon the observation of a debased mythological tradition; inasmuch as the tradition is debased, by so much have the standards of society been reduced. Thus, in "Late Afternoon in Manzanillo" Doctor Faustus and Saint Luke have become money-grubbing bourgeoisie, the Messiah has been reduced to a malaria-raddled "Jesusito," Jason has been transformed into the captain of a fishing boat, and his quest is now for one of the local prostitutes. Similarly, in "a small port in the outer fijis" the poet makes an ironic social commentary by observing the extent to which a heroic tradition has been rendered shabby. In the modern world, mythology can become a parody of itself; the traditional nobility of tone and the stirring imagery can become bastardized. In "a small port in the outer fijis" the Sea Chief is "Tunaboat Captain Sato," who "will sing ... his voyage" upon the theme of catfood, shark fins and international tuna poaching. His audience consists of "Chief Cannery & his Lady" and the "Paramount Chiefs," an Australian harbor master and a New Zealand fishmeal merchant.

Birney's romantic sense of history and mythology are also offended in a city like Cartagena, where all is squalor and petty thievery. As in "Captain Cook" or *Trial of a City* he seems to feel that the violence of the past in some way was jusified because it was wholehearted, daring, even dignified. "Gems and indigo" are at least more exotic plunder than "Old Golds unexcised." Drake, Cole, and Morgan may have been pirates and plunderers but they and their Indian opponents provide a more dramatic portrait than the current crop of bourgeois tourists being pestered by hucksters with contraband watches and cigarettes. The same observation of a debased mythology underlies "Toronto Board of Trade goes abroad," in which Birney rings some changes on the story of Dives and Lazarus. Here Lazarus represents the whole human race, narrowly resurrected from extinction by a political decision, while Dives (the speaker) pleads in a multiplicity of ironies for a drink of "clean" water from "good old LAKE ONTARIO."

Birney's evocation of mythological references is not always satirical, however. He often uses myth and fable to relate modern-days events to archetypal experience. Some of the earliest examples of this technique can be found in his poems about the onset of World War II. Both "Vancouver Lights" and "In this Verandah" reach back to the fabulous past for images that will be adequate to express the poet's awareness of onrushing disaster. The imagery of "Vancouver Lights" suggests the cyclical pattern in the affairs of men, of grand achievement followed by wretched disaster. It is an expression of pride in man's ability to raise a Camelot at the same time that it acknowledges the probable victory of the forces of darkness in man's spirit. The ordinary Canadian soldiers and airmen going to meet their fates in Europe are linked to the heroes of history and prehistory by the rhythmic click and snip of knitting needles and scissors in some insignificant Toronto verandah.

The use of myth to link men of disparate backgrounds and to bring the past alive for them can be seen in "Machu Picchu," where four tourists of quite different backgrounds develop a feeling of awe and kinship not just for each other but for the ancient Incas who built the mysterious city. Birney laces the poem with references to Druids, Christians, and Germanic witches and ties these various threads to the timelessness of Machu Picchu and the sun-worshipers who built it. As he points out, Hiram Bingham must have been sustained by a belief in myth to continue his search for a city which he was not even sure existed. The power of myth overcomes Birney and his companions as well when they actually set foot in the silent city:

> But the truth is our talk was mainly
> to hide how we felt growing suddenly
> bodily back into legend. . . .

Birney himself is "stirred / by quite nameless excitement" as he realizes that the city itself is a monument to human stubbornness and perseverance. He began his visit to Machu Picchu doubting the merits or even the significance of these two qualities, but he ends it recognizing that they can be the stuff of fable and that their fabulous quality can link men across barriers of time and space. Some day Machu Picchu will crumble away like everything else but until that far-distant day it will provide a rallying point for the human spirit.

Birney does something similar in "Pachucan Miners," where three different mythological traditions are used to frame and lend dimension and meaning to the labor of modern-day silver miners. A basic irony exists in the fact that the silver ore is free to enjoy sun and fresh air while the miners themselves are slaves of darkness:

> the ore has risen
> into the tasselled wind and run
> on singing rails beneath the ardent
> sky to sorceries beyond vision.

Yet, both miners and prostitutes play their assigned roles "without rancour," as is becoming of gods who know that they are beyond the grasp of mere earthly things. They know that each night they will effect a heroic rescue — of themselves as men, of their pre-Columbian traditions, and of their knowledge of themselves as a race. They emerge from their captivity in the mine "like a defeated army," but as they descend into their own village they regain strength from the past:

> backs fling upright, O now legs are male,
> are braced, each knotty pair, to hold
> up song and hurl it at the night,
> then step their own way down to where
> deep in her torchy den,
> snakes Toltecan looping in her ears,
> her crucifix agleam above the sheets,
> Euridice reclines and hears
> the wild guitars, and daily waits
> the nightly rescue of her silver men.

If Birney is aware of the omnipresence of myth in everyday life, he is also aware that all too often it is overwhelmed by modern technology or ignored in favor of shallow contemporary preoccupations. A poem like "Transistor," for example, has all the elements of a quest story: Birney has sought out the witch in her remote sanctuary, has been guided safely to her by the engineer who also knows the magic verbal formula that will make her reveal her treasure, and has crossed her palm with golden rum so that she will help unlock the mystery of his own humanity. As she sings it becomes clear that she is only the medium by which a message is being transmitted to Birney and in fact to anyone else who is willing to search out his kinship with the human race. But the old woman's own people are not interested in her magic or her wisdom; they are distracted by the yodeling of some Caribbean cowboy singing stale hits from last year's Top of the Pops. Birney recognizes that he and they are doing essentially the same thing; they are all trying to relate their own lives to a larger segment of humanity, but one cannot help feeling that the scrawny old black woman lends a dimension to her magic that the cheap transistor radio cannot.

A somewhat similar situation occurs in "Tavern by the Hellespont," where Birney sits musing about the fact that modern man can only articulate his mythology in technological terms. The two American tourists are astonished by the cleverness of the fortune-teller but the only simile that will serve to express their delight is "her priestess eyes / are doubly real as television." As for Birney, sitting alone with his thoughts in a place of great historical significance, the only reality, in fact the dominant reality, is the radio playing somewhere in the background. All the mystery of the past and the magic of the present are subservient to an electronic device.

Finally, there is Birney's mythology of the future, a mythology used to project a horrifying vision of a raddled planet inhabited by cockroaches and deformed human beings. The questing poet in the twenty-first century will find himself in a landscape as barren as the moon or Australia's outback, peopled by savages who ignore the import of their own artifacts as they scrabble for survival. Some of them like the "conceivable great grandson" will sport various deformities resulting from nuclear radiation; in other words, the human race is preparing its own supply of monsters against the day when technology will have killed off any belief in the comparatively innocent trolls and sprites of ancient times. Nor will the poet, if one still exists, have an easy time of it since, after all, he will be not nearly so well equipped for survival as is the cockroach.

All of this, of course, will be the logical outcome of the situation described in "November Walk Near False Creek Mouth" in which a series of played-out myths is used as a metaphor for Birney's belief that mankind is a degenerate species only awaiting the final holocaust. It is, in fact, in the "November" of its tenure on earth; as Frank Davey observed,

here, then, is the "twilight of the gods," of all the gods. But unlike the Norse Götterdämmerung, this twilight of baleful omens sees as yet no violence, no energy of plot and counterplot. All gods are debased and moribund, and the people await the last explosion with languorous acquiescence.[9]

The question might also be raised as to whether Birney has not cast himself in the role of a modern-day Gulliver, roaming about the earth and recording his encounters with various marvelous creatures. His Brobdignagians would clearly be those heroic figures like Cook, Conrad Kain, David and the Salish chief, all large of spirit, bold, and questing and yet essentially peaceful in their characters. The Lilliputians would be those petty spirits like Mr. Chubb, the Toronto Board of Trade member, or the speaker in "Billboards Build Freedom of Choice," men and women who fritter away their lives in wrangling over financial gain or political advantage. The residents of Laputa and Balnibarbi are clearly present; one has only to read "1984 minus 17 & counting at u of waterloo" or "messy-jests for a kinageing kitchmess" to catch a glimpse of their handi-work. But who then are Birney's Houyhnhnms? There do not seem to be any. Perhaps Birney thinks that the earth never really would produce a race of creatures guided by pure intelligence and reason, or possibly he left them out of his scheme of things because they reminded him too strongly of the academic community: rational yet limited and narrow-minded, condescending, and insufferably sanctimonious.

In summation, then, it might be said that Birney's interest in myth is an indication of his belief in a heroic or romantic past. It is perhaps also a product of his own struggles with titanic foes, including mountains that had to be climbed and political movements that had to be supported in his vigorous youth, to say nothing of his experience of World War II, where perhaps for the last time in history it appeared that the forces of right were aligned against a demonic foe. By the same token, the mythic images that characterize many of the war poems in *Now Is Time* and *Strait of Anian* were later turned to ironic or satiric purpose as Birney's view of mankind and the future of the world became increasingly embittered. The rather wistfully optimistic use of the Christmas story in an early poem like "Christmas Comes" would later be transformed into a virulent Jeremiad in "kitchmess day cure-all" and "twas 8 nights before kitchmess."

Then there is the matter of Birney's apparent lack of belief in the existence of a Canadian mythology. Milton Wilson has referred to Birney as a "Canadian gleeman with an empty mythhoard,"[10] a fact which may account to some extent for Birney's incessant roaming. Once he has finished contemplating the Canadian scenery, as in "Reverse on the Coast Range" or "Page of Gaspé," and the Canadian people, as in "Anglosaxon Street" or "Toronto Board of Trade Goes Abroad," and has built as many mythological references into these poems as he can, he feels that he must go abroad in search of what is missing in an historically and mythically empty land.

This sense of the lack of an indigenous mythological tradition is shared by other poets like Douglas Le Pan in poems like "A Country Without a Mythology," and yet some poets like E. J. Pratt have found the stuff of heroic tradition in the lives of the Jesuit missionaries and the builders of the railroads. Perhaps Pratt was able to see things in Canada's geography and history that Birney and Le Pan overlooked. For one thing the vastness of the Canadian landscape tends to absorb Canadian writers and to diminish the relative importance of their work. Moreover, Canadians have tended to be too busy building and exploiting their country to establish a literary tradition or a mythology. All of this Birney acknowledges in poems like "can. lit.," and yet even as he makes this acknowledgment he reveals himself to be typically Canadian in ignoring the heroic accomplishments of some Canadians, including those who opened the West, explored the Arctic, and fought in various wars.

One of the paradoxes in Birney's work, then, is that he is typically Canadian in believing that Canada has no real body of myth to draw upon; we may never have one since we now live, in Dan Wakefield's phrase, in a "fact-smothered era." On the other hand, Birney's own background and inclinations keep leading him back to mythology as one of the few adequate means of expressing his sense of the grandeur of the natural world and the heroic element in the human spirit. If he has accepted the idea that there is no native mythological tradition in Canada, then he is perfectly willing to go abroad or back into time to borrow what he needs from various foreign traditions and adapt them both to his own requirements as a Canadian and as a citizen of the modern world.

201968

CHAPTER 5

Nature Poetry

FROM his very earliest years Birney began acquiring a fund of knowledge about the natural world upon which he was to draw for poetic material during the remainder of his life. His early years on the farm near Lacombe, often alone with his mother, exposed him to the life of the foothills, and his youth spent in Banff and the Rockies provided him with an intimate knowledge of the mountains. Even as a child he must have been a careful observer of the natural world; he does not remember his mother's garden as containing just "flowers" as most children would, but "morning glories, candytuft [and] mignonette," and he wanted "some of Mrs. Bell's sweet william." All this before he was seven. He says that by the time the Birneys moved back to Calgary in 1911, "Nature, if she had not marked me for her own, had certainly put a bony finger on me, and I was never to accommodate myself to pavement.... Bird and beast were ... my early tutors, especially the latter."[1]

As for the inanimate part of the natural world, Birney's knowledge acquired in childhood and youth and especially the knowledge he gained during the two years that he worked in the mountains prior to entering university was reinforced by the science courses which he took before he switched to English Literature in his second year. Thus, the testimony of Professor E. O. seen in *The Damnation of Vancouver,* for example, as well as the accurate references to flora and fauna throughout Birney's poetry are reflections of Birney's careful study of the world around him. Even during his summers spent on the islands in the Gulf of Georgia away from his teaching duties at the University of British Columbia Birney seized every opportunity to perfect this knowledge; for three of those summers he made a hobby of collecting marine invertebrates and at one point sought professional help in identifying these animals from sketches he had made.

There is much of Birney in David, who is able to identify the mountain animals and plants and who is familiar with the geological formations, just as there is something of Birney in the portrait of Conrad Kain, the unlettered mountaineer who "lectured on rocks like a don / or spoke of birds as if one himself." Birney's poems are filled with scornful references to university teachers, men crammed with knowledge learned from books; to him, the best knowledge is that acquired from contact with nature. He takes it almost as a point of honor to familiarize himself with the flora and fauna of every region that he visits.

This knowledge has paid rich dividends in Birney's poetry. His familiarity with the Rockies permitted him to move mountains around at will in order to get them into the locus of the action of "David"; some he renamed to suit his own purposes, others, like "the Finger," he invented.[3] His mastery of the terrain is revealed in the fact that for years critics and mountaineers have been searching for and discovering the "true" location of David's fall.

Birney's carefully observed and dispassionate portraits of the natural world began with his very earliest poems; in "Kootenay Still-life," for example, the landscape, the broken tree, the crow, and the mouse are all frozen in a moment of time. Here, as in "Poem," death is part of the landscape, but since the killing of a mouse by a crow or the dolphin eating flying fish are part of the normal functioning of nature, Birney suspends his usually ironic commentary and records the scene simply as it exists. "Poem" has ironic implications for mankind and for man's various religious beliefs, but it is also a sharply etched portrait of one of the cycles of the natural world. "Oldster" is another poem where irony is replaced by affectionate whimsy; the accurate description of the aging process in a poplar tree — scaly bark, broken branches, moss — is counterpointed by the humorous suggestion that the old tree will have to be "dueled" down by some young man looking for firewood, and by the comforting knowledge that the tree has already sired his progeny, "grandsons of green" to succeed him when he is gone.

The early habit of paying careful attention to what he sees and of taking pains to learn the names and characteristics of flowers, birds, trees, and animals is continued in Birney's later poems like "Caribbean Kingdoms" and "perth, australia, i love you." "Caribbean Kingdoms" is a portrait of tranquil and unconscious beauty on a par with "Slug in Woods"; the moral which Birney urges in the poem — that unconscious nature has a power superior to that of sentient creatures — is almost lost in the dazzling array of hibiscus, jasmine, roses, and arums. Something similar is true of "perth, australia, i love you." Birney, as in most of the poems in *what's so big about GREEN?,* is grumbling bitterly about imminent nuclear destruction, pollution, and the world's disregard of its poets, but all the harsh commentary is subdued by the beauty of the poet's description of the city:

> but meantime here's You in your September spring
> a launching pad for botanists on space-trip
> a happening in spice & rainbows
> a young witch gardening
> between Outback & empty Ocean....

The catalogue of flowers and trees, of birds and reptiles, overwhelms the reader with a sense of the quiet power of nature; Birney's bitter Jeremiad is hushed and absorbed by the embrace of nature's glories.

When it comes to writing poetry about nature, Birney's lapses are so rare that they only serve to illuminate the accuracy of his work as a whole; for example, the sumac tine is not magenta in the springtime, as he suggests in "Quebec May." Still, set over against poems like "Slug in Woods" or "Takkakaw Falls" or any of Birney's dozens of other nature poems, such shortcomings are insignificant. In the same volume which saw the publication of "Quebec May" and "Laurentian Shield" (*Strait of Anian*) one finds a poem like "Prairie Counterpoint" that contains lines as lyrical as anything that Keats ever wrote:

> The harebell swings in the moon.
> The morning-glory blows
> white trumpets to the rose
> and scented saskatoon
> The bearded buffalo go
> like Israelites under the sun.
> . . . .
> A coyote in a trance of fraud
> warps toward the grouse's flock.

Here as elsewhere, Birney's descriptions of the natural world are among his very finest poems.

I *Man and Nature*

It has been said that "Birney accepts what Malcolm Lowry averred in one of his notebooks: that the essential centre of Canada is its consciousness of the wildernesss...."[4] This may be true for Birney, but his poetry tends to bear witness to his dismay at the lack of consciousness of the wilderness on the part of his fellow Canadians and the eagerness with which Canadians embrace urban life. From the sleepy prairie dwellers of "Winter Saturday" through the city-bound "Climbers" to the grit and dirt of a "Sunday Nightfall in Winnipeg" and the smug boosterism of "Toronto Board of Trade Goes Abroad" there is a broad trail of poems devoted to the Canadian's fear or ignorance of the wilderness.

Northrop Frye, of course, had Birney's poetry in mind when he said that

...the outstanding achievement of Canadian poetry is in the evocation of stark terror. Not a coward's terror, of course; but a controlled vision of the causes of cowardice. The immediate source of this is obviously the frightening loneliness of a huge and thinly settled country. When all the intelligence, morality, reverence and simian cunning of man confronts a sphinx-like riddle of the indefinite like the Canadian winter the man seems as helpless as a trapped mink and lonely as a loon. His thrifty little heaps of civilized values look pitiful beside nature's apparently meaningless power to waste and destroy on a superhuman scale...."[5]

This comment perfectly sums up the greatest virtues, the laudable essence, of "David," "Bushed," "Atlantic Door," "Laurentian Shield," and a whole host of Birney's other poems, all of which contain the motif of man making moral and ethical demands: for order, for sympathy, for comfort, of a vast, harsh country that is totally indifferent to so weak and defenseless a creature. And from this in turn springs the element of animism in Birney's poetry, the element which derives from the characters' desire to attribute their misfortunes to a conscious power. As Frye goes on to say, "Nature is seen by the poet, first as unconsciousness, then as a kind of existence which is cruel and meaningless, then as the source of the cruelty and subconscious stampedings within the human mind." For Frye, Canadians have very little of the tendency to come to terms with and live in harmony with nature that is found in the works of American writers,[6] as for example in Whitman, Thoreau, and even Hemingway.

Birney says that, when he wrote "David" in 1940, "I had to unburden myself about mountains...;" he felt a compulsion to verbalize his own experiences in the Rockies and to express his sense of their beauty and their hostility.[7] The concept of nature's active hostility emerges after David's fall from the Finger; the Wordsworthian idyll is suddenly transformed into a Canadian deathtrap: ... the snow is "sun-cankered," the crevasses are "gaping" and "greenthroated," the seracs are "fanged," the glacier has a "snout." Even on more solid ground the swamp that had earlier "quivered with frogsong" is now "ragged" and its toadstools are "obscene." The landscape has come alive; it is no longer an ocean but a body, the body of a vampire or cannibal or ghoul.... David's fall into death is the narrator's fall into a vision of Nature as a destructive and hideous monster.[8]

The fact that this vision of nature is a projection of the human mind is seen more clearly in a poem like "Bushed," which is ostensibly about a man who goes mad and becomes "bushed," living alone in the mountains, but which in fact deals with the impossibility of the average human mind to comprehend the awesome indifference of nature or to exist for long in its presence. Nature's apparent malignancy is a projection of the observer's mentality and results from a sense of guilt and fear in the presence of a power that he cannot influence, much less control. Even David and Conrad Kain, however sane they might be, are only momentary intruders; and one of them is destroyed, while the other's finest boast is that he managed to keep his parties safe from harm in the mountains. David's qualities are as futile in the face of an indifferent nature as are those of the dead lawyer in "ARRIVALS — Wolfville" whose

> longfingered hand
> stretched in some arresting habit of eloquence
> to the last irrational judgment
> roaring in from the storm.

The sense of terror at being alone in the presence of nature is dealt with specifically in "leaving the Park." Instead of being in harmony with it, man feels that nature must be "barred," "limited," shut out of mind; the park is a sort of natural ghetto, safe enough to drive through by day but something which must be avoided at all costs by night. The beauty and tranquillity of the park are a standing reproach to frenetic and destructive mankind to whom even the moon represents "a bright noose." To escape the sensations of guilt and terror they will "hurry a long way / and pay to camp."

A variation on this theme occurs in "Atlantic Door" and "Maritime Faces," where man is reminded that although he may cross the ocean for "gain or solace," i.e., although he has gained some degree of mastery over the element which spawned him, he must not forget that that element remains indifferent and ruthless. Birney is aware of the ocean's beauty but he does not seek to dramatize that aspect; on the contrary, he derives a *memento mori* philosophy from its indifference. In "Maritime Faces" he suggests that man can survive in the natural world by being eternally vigilant — David forgot this rule for a moment and perished — and by integrating himself with nature; he must become hardened and watchful like the rocky maritime hills crouching at the edge of the Atlantic. The suggestion here, as in "Climbers," is that man must find the solutions to his problems himself; if he experiences terror at the sight of the lonely face of nature then he must seek out a solution to that terror in his own character. The climbers, like the seafarers, must recognize that nature consists of the impersonal sea or the "pointless points of the peaks" and that this impersonality can prove to be a terrifying mirror in which are reflected the shortcomings of any man who has not prepared himself to meet the challenges of the natural world.

Although Birney often dwells upon the theme of a terrifying natural world, he also is capable of showing nature to be in some ways more rational than man. In poems like "And the Earth Grow Young Again," "Invasion Spring," and "D-Day" nature's warfare is seen as necessary and justifiable, in contrast to mankind's pointless killing; the birds of prey kill only in order to eat. What is more, nature works incessantly to repair the damage caused by mankind's wars; the fireweed covers a bombhole and the finches use the radar tinsel to reinforce their nests just as the oak trees have successfully obliterated the traces of Caesar's armies. In the contrast between this continuous and interlocking process of destruction and rebirth on the part of nature and man's purely destructive wars, mankind acquires the characteristics usually attributed to "irrational" nature.

Sometimes Birney treats the theme of nature's "warfare" in a whimsical manner. The trees along the Pacific coast which he had seen as vigilant and even menacing soldiers in "Captain Cook" are treated as comic-opera characters in "Reverse on the Coast Range," where a natural disaster is playfully recast as a military operation. The larches are forced to kneel in the face of "the wind that machinegunned down from the peak" and both the hemlock "reserves" and the "veteran battalions of Alpine fir" are routed by the avalanche's "broadside." While this disaster is being inflicted upon one part of the tree population, another part, farther away in the safety of the seacoast, continues to indulge itself like careless civilians amusing themselves far from the scene of a battle. The dogwood flee from danger "clutching / The dreams of their waxen vanities," while the madrona continues to tan its "lazy limbs" and the maples, like pregnant women, dream of the life that is stirring within them.

The whimsical treatment of nature as a power unconquered by its own destructive forces and only slightly disturbed by those of man is continued in "toronto march" and "in purdy's ameliasburg." "Toronto march" is a poem in the style of Simon and Garfunkel's "Silent Night," i.e., excerpts from the news announcing various manmade disasters counterpoint the observations that everywhere in the world nature is busy renewing itself: flowers are blooming, buds are bursting, young are being born, and that nature will stubbornly continue with this process even though man seems determined to obliterate himself. This same theme, in a slightly lower key, is found in "in purdy's ameliasburg," where the horrors of urban life and the encroachments of developers and summer cottagers are forgotten in the tranquil beauty of a rural springtime. The empty winebottle, the dandelions, the heron, and Purdy's private mouse bowing from the kitchen floor place the threatening "civilized" world in a diminished perspective.

Birney's wry affection and respect for the natural world can even be seen in poems like "cucarachas in fiji," "Slug in Woods," and "Bushed." He has to confess a grudging admiration for the stinking, bothersome cockroach because of its infinitely greater ability to survive than that of man. If Birney's grandchildren survive the nuclear holocaust and come to repopulate Fiji they still will be faced with the problem of a new and better cockroach, ten feet long "& spraying humanicide from every tentacle." The evocation of verdant peace in "Slug in Woods" suggests that Birney holds an affection for this lowly creature who is "himself his viscid wife," that he does not extend to mankind, just as his sympathy seems to lie with the gruff old ogre of a mountain in "Bushed" rather than with the loony trapper who invades the mountain's demesne.

This tone of sympathy with nature is a reflection of a phenomenon that Margaret Atwood has commented upon:

A curious thing starts happening in Canadian literature once man starts winning [the battle against Nature]. Sympathy begins to shift from the victorious hero to the defeated giantess, and the problem is no longer how to avoid being swallowed up by a cannibalistic Nature but how to avoid destroying her.[9]

If man is defeated by nature, as Bob is in "David" or the trapper is in "Bushed," he is in some way weak or neurotic or reprehensible, but if he defeats nature, as in "the mammoth corridors," he is an exploiter or ravager of natural beauty.

The damage done by human exploitation of the natural world is fully documented in Birney's poetry. "Slug in Woods" suggests that nature without man has certain inherent dangers but nothing to compare with those displayed in "Images in Place of Logging" or "Transcontinental." The sustained sea imagery of "Slug in Woods" suggests the quiet of the ocean floor; nature is alone and unspoiled, killing only in order to feed and then dispassionately, whereas "Images in Place of Logging" illustrates man's penchant for destroying natural beauty. Birney is fond of the tree-as-soldier image and uses it in various contexts. In "Alaska Passage" and "Captain Cook" the trees are sentries in a world of nature versus man where the chances of victory are at least equal for either side. In "Reverse on the Coast Range" the trees are defeated soldiers in a situation that pits nature against itself. But in "Images in Place of Logging" the trees are massacred nonconformists in a war of man against nature. The "pacifist firs" and "spruce resisters" finally have to lift their hands "to revolver sun" while the place where they lived is converted into a monstrous charnelhouse for their kin: the crisscrossed logs resemble the crosses in a cemetery while the fireweed provides wreathes for the "tombs of the roots."

A similar contrast can be drawn between "Takkakaw Falls" and "what's so big about GREEN?" In the former the river tumbles and crashes to its death but eventually, after a spell in purgatory, regenerates itself and rises anew. In the latter poem the emphasis is upon the irreversible result of man's victory over nature. The lake that had existed for thousands of years is now dead, destroyed beyond possibility of redemption by man's assault.

After the first attack the lake fought back and "almost won," but man renewed his assault upon nature and in "four generations / made organic death at last / an irreversible reaction." In the natural world, as Birney observed in "Hands," the battle is "steeped in silence / the fallen have use and fragrantly nourish the quick" but mankind's "roots are in autumn and store for no spring."

Then there is the question of how man and specifically a poet can come to grips with the natural world in a country as vast as Canada; the sheer size, to say nothing of the diversity, of that world practically defies the human imagination. One British critic contends that in the ex-colonies which have more or less suppressed indigenous native life and artistic expression there is a tendency to try to come to grips with nature by personifying it. The Canadians, especially, often go out of their way to deal with the whole huge country as a unified entity.[10] This may be wishful thinking on the part of the poets in the face of geographical and political facts but it is also a reaction to the problem that Northrop Frye identified when he said that in E. J. Pratt's *Toward the Last Spike* there is no action in the poem sufficient to support an epic theme: "the real quest is for physical and spiritual communication within [Canadian] society," and that "...here the real dragon to be killed is dead already: the obstacle is the torpor and inertia of unconscious nature...."[11]

Birney attempts to deal with these various aspects of the same problem by writing wide-ranging poems like "North Star West" and the "Transcanada" series, by attributing a certain animism to nature, as in "David" or "Bushed," and by superimposing an imported mythology upon various areas of the country, as in "Laurentian Shield," "David," and "Atlantic Door." The bird's-eye view from the aircraft in "North Star West" is only partially successful in providing a cohesive impression of the country; ultimately the poet has to resort to a series of poems on the various regions of Canada just as he resorts to the same device in dealing with another large country, Mexico. In other words, no one, including Birney, has yet managed to encompass what may be called the Canadian experience in a single poem.

If the size of the natural world is a problem for the poet, so is the question of how to put man back into touch with nature, to re-awaken in him a sense of kinship with it and to make him see himself as an integral part of that world. Birney feels that he himself has not always been successful in trying to put himself in sympathy with the natural world. On the one hand, he recalls seeing the innumerable wandering cows, crows, monkeys, and rats of India, all of which were a considerable nuisance to the Indians but which the Indians thought of as fellow creatures and, in Ghandi's phrase, "poems of pity."[12] Something of this attitude informs poems like "The Bear on the Delhi Road" and "Slug in Woods," where the wild creatures hold center stage and man, if he is present at all, is relegated to a secondary role.

Just as often, however, Birney admits that man has lost the aboriginal ability to unify himself with nature. In "the mammoth corridors" he says that the first Indians working their way down the continent from Asia and the Bering Strait moved "Swinging westward then over howling summits / to possess these still fresh-hewn alps / (which I inheriting do not possess)," and "First Tree for Frost" is a wry confession of his failure to understand both nature and human character. "Winter Saturday" is just one of the many poems in which he underlines man's lack of awareness of the world around him. The people in the poem are like the slug in the forest; they come out of their cocoon momentarily to search for pleasure as instinctively as the slug searches for food but with just as little awareness or sympathy for the world around them. Despite the fact that the wilderness constantly impinges upon the Canadian consciousness, Canadians still tend to be ignorant of it, or if they are aware of it they see it as a hostile environment, something to be overthrown and tamed.

II *Nature as Symbol*

Not only does the natural world provide the subject for many of Birney's poems, it also is a source of images and symbols that recur throughout his work. Consciously or unconsciously he has come to use the sea, the mountains, the prairies, certain animals, trees, and, most of all, the sun as symbols of larger forces in the affairs of men.

Of these various elements, the sea is one that recurs with great frequency in Birney's poetry. In "Mappemounde" and "Captain Cook" it represents a highway for the questing human spirit; in "Gulf of Georgia" it is the source of life; in "Atlantic Door," a symbol of strength and vigor; in "November Walk Near False Creek Mouth," "Vancouver Lights," and "Dusk on the Bay" it is a source of tranquillity and repose conducive to profound thought, and in "Wake Island" it symbolizes nature's patience in the face of man's troubling.

The sea also provides the governing image in poems like "still," "Slug in Woods," and "The Ebb Begins from Dream." In "still" the speaker's preoccupation with his lover is represented by the ceaseless swirling of an eddy around a rock, while "Slug in Woods" is a development of the concept of the atmosphere as an ocean. The slug moving across the floor like a marine creature moving across the floor of the ocean in a way represents the unity of all living things; every creature exists in an ocean of air or of water, and although that ocean is a beneficient and life-giving element it is also constricting, setting limits upon the creature's ability to move and to achieve. Hence the image of man or beast attempting to rise out of that element, like the flying fish in "Poem" or the poet in "North Star West":

> A forty ton bubble we rise, rise,
> break through clouds like rollers
> burst to sunlight. . . .

This is a metaphor for the upward striving of all orders of life, and specifically for man's struggles to rise out of intellectual darkness.

In "The Ebb Begins from Dream," the rhythm of human affairs is equated with the rhythm of the tides. From the high-water mark of comfort, sleep, and absence of care, man is pulled remorselessly down into the waking world of daily routine: jobs, domestic matters, striving for ideals which never seem to be attained, and then at the end of the day is swept wearily back up onto the beach to seek in sleep a surcease from the world of failed ideals and ceaseless troubling. This poem is in some ways a milder, sadder, more thoughtful reworking of the satire in "Anglosaxon Street," another poem whose underlying pattern is that of tidal motion.

Birney uses the sea as metaphor and as symbol over and over again in *Down the Long Table*. As the book opens, the middle-aged Gordon Saunders reflects upon the manner in which his life is linked with the lives of all other men throughout the ages; in a line reminiscent of the closing lines of "Atlantic Door" Saunders realizes that his past was formed by the ocean of human experience and that the story of his life is destined to become part of that same shaping experience. Later in the book, the youthful Gordon Saunders attempts to express his concept of social order in terms of the ocean and swimmers; when he is shouted down by the party members who fear him as an original thinker he storms out of the meeting hall and dives into the night air like a swimmer who dives into cold water. The shock of the moment causes him to reflect upon the tranquillity of the night and the falling snow like dead matter drifting toward the bottom of the sea; for him the carelessly falling snow becomes a metaphor for nature's indifference to man's petty politicking. To the very end, however, Gordon thinks of political activists as swimmers striving against inertia to reach a better shore.

The sea is not always a benign image in Birney's poetry. Sometimes, as in "Maritime Faces," "Atlantic Door," and "Wake Island," it represents the indifference or even the active hostility of nature to man. In "Maritime Faces" the sea is cast as a bully, battering man and landscape in a tireless effort to overcome them both. In "Atlantic Door" and "Wake Island" the emphasis is upon the ocean as representative of nature's uncaring attitude toward mankind; man may make his way successfully over the empty wastes of the Atlantic or even the Pacific but in the end he is less significant than a morning glory seed which has made the same voyage and probably will do so again once man has finished destroying himself. The "capacious tombs of the sea" stand as a permanent reminder to man of his own mortality, for they remind him incessantly of the wastes of eternity into which someday he must fall.

If the sea symbolizes various things in Birney's poetry, sometimes comforting and womblike, sometimes harsh and menacing, the sun has a consistently beneficent image. To Birney it represents everything that is good: life, warmth, growth, comfort. From his earliest years he was a sun-worshiper, perhaps because of his childhood experience of the Canadian winter. From about the age of seven he remembers: "Sunday School — Mother's big hat — Jesus loves me, etc — wanting to be a missionary in China — Beatitudes and Twenty First Psalm — hating to go inside out of the sunshine ('You in your dark corner')...."[13] It is impossible to read any amount of Birney's work without becoming aware of the warmth/cold duality in the imagery and of Birney's devotion to the sun.

This devotion can be seen most clearly in the two poems "song for sunsets" and "daybreak on lake opal." In "song for sunsets" the sun is "big dad" and "the one who never sleeps," but Birney also expresses the anxiety of primitive man, who saw the sun disappearing at night and was never sure if it would reappear in the morning. Like a child trying to protect himself from loneliness, he tells the sun exactly where to find him next morning:

> goodnite sun
> im turning over again
> im on the little ball
> so slowly rolling
> backwards from you. . . .

But even then he is not sure that the sun will actually reappear; he can only "hope" it will be there and "trust" that he will be able to find his own way back to it in the morning, for at the center of the poem lies the knowledge that his love is not reciprocated; the sun is too busy taking care of the whole solar system to notice one man or even a whole race of men.

It is very tempting to refer to "daybreak on lake opal" as the companion poem to "song for sunsets," although they have never been set in print in such a way as to suggest that this is the case. Still, Birney has read them in public as companion-pieces and their themes are clearly complementary. Where "song for sunsets" strikes the anxious note of a child being separated from a loving parent, "daybreak on lake opal" is a joyous greeting of that parent upon his return in the morning. Where the sun-worship in "song for sunsets" is tempered by a knowledge of the sun's ultimate indifference, in "daybreak on lake opal" it is marked by a splendid dignity. The poem is actually a hymn to be chanted to the returning sun, bringing back life to the "scarred for/-ever-by-the-wind-besieged/ ramparts the icecracked tree-/ breached walls."

Birney often deals with the experience of war in terms of sun and cold. "Hands" strike the autumnal note of a race that is preoccupied with killing, and "War Winters" develops the motif. In the latter poem the sun is a metaphor for the human heart, capable of great warmth, love, and creativity, but now grown pale, distant, and impotent because of the icy season besetting the human race; the "proud Bessemer, peltwarmer, beauty" has become a "tarnished chimneyplug," a "sucked wafer," a "white simpleton." The miseries of the present wretched winter are not so much a result of natural laws ruling our solar system as they are of man's folly; the ice is in the heart as much as it is in the rivers and lakes. This metaphor recurs in Birney's agonized picture of wartime Holland in

"The Road to Nijmegen," with its imagery of frost, starvation, destruction, and death. Into this bleak portrait there streams only one ray of warmth: the power of the human heart; only love can provide the "light of kindness" that will lead mankind, Lazarus-like, back from the grave.

Birney also uses the sun as a symbol of youthful idealism, passion, and romantic love. In *Down the Long Table* Gordon Saunders is at times aware of the callowness of his actions and the cynical outlook of hard-line party members, but he still feels that he has acted rightly; like Stephen Spender he has been "looking for men born of the sun, so that [he may] travel a little way with them toward the sun."[14] Even the sordid death of one of the men he had taken for an ally and the collapse of his efforts to organize Vancouver cannot quench that belief. On the same note, Birney urges the little Bangkok boy to "Prance / this dazzled instant / of your father's big / Buddha smile." The future, for the boy, is cold, foreboding, filled with chalk-faced tourists and deadening labor where the boy must slide "lethewards" down and away from the sun, but for the moment he can give a "cry / of joy under / the sun!"

A logical corollary of using the sun as a symbol of all that is benign and creative in the world is to use images of cold, snow, and the winter to suggest everything sterile and malign. Hence the suggestion of impending disaster in the opening lines of "October in Utah" as the tokens of Indian Summer are put to flight by the wintry wind. The same atmosphere develops in "David"; as the summer wanes and David moves toward his death, the *memento mori* signals accumulate. As the poem opens, the mountains are "steps to the sun's retreats," but as the summer advances the young men come upon the skeleton of a mountain goat, the tracks of a grizzly — always a symbol of nature's ferocity in Birney's poetry — "by the lowest snow," and finally the injured robin (a bird of summer). In the end they make their ill-fated assault upon the Finger "under the cold / Breath of the glacier." The cold shadow that creeps toward Bob as he lies beside the crippled David suggests the shadow of death, or the chilling decision that Bob must take alone now that David's sunny spirit is quenched.

Images of cold are also used in "the gray woods exploding" and "Reading the diary" to symbolize death, grief, lost love. When Birney meets the "young-old" English professor in "the gray woods exploding" for the first time the atmosphere is bleak with references to "October's wind," snow, stalactites, and the sense of "an always-too-early-fall." As the poem unfolds with its tale of treachery, suffering, disillusionment, and mourning, Birney realizes that the chill atmosphere emanates from his host, whose spirit has been blighted by his experience of life. "Reading the diary," with its theme of a young person struggling against social pressures and wartime anxieties to be free to develop as a human being and as an artist, is cast in terms of a young tree's efforts to burst from the seed and then to grow to maturity in the face of the "Iceland in the breath." "Branch-broken, frost-nipped," the young tree can only survive through the long winter of the war by "believing in summer."

The two companion poems "Man Is a Snow" and "...Or a Wind" are classic examples of Birney's use of snow, cold, ice, and frost to symbolize destructiveness, pessimism, blindness, and sterility in man, while the sun represents hope, creativity, intelligence, and optimism. In the first poem man's ability to appreciate the beauty of the natural world and to see into the realm of dreams and myth is obscured by the frost in the soul, and man himself is depicted as a snow that smothers and stifles his own ability to love. On the other hand, "...Or a Wind" suggests that although mankind is as frustrated in its search for peace as a wind battering against a cliff, yet, "while the sun [or life]" exists there remains the hope that the cliff may be breached and the breath of life may blow freely over the future. It is tempting to note the places of composition of these two poems and to think that they represent Birney's inmost reaction to natural phenomena; the pessimism of "Man Is a Snow" may reflect the gloomy November of 1946 in Vancouver while the optimism of "...Or a Wind" may have been inspired by a sunny June day on Bowen Island.

Another important source of nature imagery is found in the mountain-flatland opposition in Birney's poetry. The prairie and tundra tend to be associated not only with the boredom and loneliness of the Canadian wilderness but with some element of evil or malice in the natural world. The mountains, on the other hand, while they too have their element of risk and danger, represent the challenge, inspiration, and beauty of nature and, in the case of the sunny Pacific slope, they represent peace, comfort, and generosity of spirit.

Birney uses the prairie as a symbol of the hostility that man senses in the natural world in poems like "Leaving the Park," where "the prying prairie" envelops and menaces the tourists who hurry nervously away from the alien beauties of Yellowstone Park and speed toward a commercial campground where they can feel at home with their own kind. In "David" Bob is conscious of the waste of "alien prairie" stretching remotely away to the east, while in "On Going to the Wars" mankind must traverse "the tundra of our dead" before it can reach the haven of the "sundrenched Pacific," and in "Man on a Tractor" the prairie and the relentless prairie winter are associated with weariness, toil, and social oppression at the same time that the mountains and the summer are linked with a life of comfort and ease.

The significance of the mountain imagery in Birney's poetry becomes clear if one contrasts the boredom implicit in poems about flat country such as "Prairie Counterpoint" and "North of Superior" with the excitement that emanates from the poems about the mountains. If there is a risk involved in challenging the mountains, there is also great beauty and possibly the satisfaction of achieving success in a gamble where one must risk one's life. Thus, Bob and David are very intensely alive when they are challenging and conquering the mountains; they are vividly aware of the beauty of the natural world and of their own vigorous response to its enticements. Similarly, the man in "Biography" who is eventually defeated by age and time begins his life by answering the challenge of the mountains. In this sense, and throughout Birney's poetry, mountains are associated with all that is grand, dangerous, and beautiful in the natural world and, by implication, with those same qualities in the human spirit. The mountains may ruthlessly extract a terrible price from those men who are weak or careless, but at the same time they offer great satisfaction, to the youthful adventurers, at least, and the best of all insights into the glories of the natural world.

Birney also attributes symbolic values to some animals in his poetry and prose. The grizzly bear, as we have seen, is nearly always representative of nature's fearsome destructive powers. Birney first used it in a short story, "The Reverend Eastham Discovers Life," in which a priggish, unforgiving, and moralistic clergyman is caught by a grizzly and killed during a walk in the Rockies. In this story the Reverend Eastham can be seen to represent man's rationalizing and moralizing character, and the bear represents the indifferent cruelty with which nature batters down man's puny arguments. A bear is also used in "halifax" to symbolize the fierce irrational side of the human character; the light roistering tone of the first and third stanzas turns harsh and gloomy at the prospect of the savage bear once again emerging from the dark caves of the human mind to begin another, and final, war. A grizzly's footprint reminds David and Bob of the ever-present menace of the natural world, and in "Time Bomb" the grizzly is once again used as a symbol of savagery and destructiveness, in nature as in man:

> In this friend's face I know
>   the grizzly still   and in the mirror
> lay my ear to the radio's conch
>   and hear the atom's terror....

If the better side of human nature is not allowed to guide the actions of the human race, then the fierce beast lurking in the spirit will surely lunge forth.

One of the most intriguing of Birney's animal symbols is that of the coyote. In very early poems like "For Steve" and "Joe Harris" Birney used the coyote as a symbol of evil, of lurking danger, guile, and duplicity. In "Joe Harris" it specifically represents the war profiteer battening on the sacrifices of the working man and in "For Steve" it represents the enemy airman. On the other hand, the coyote in poems like "In this Verandah" is a symbol of human intelligence. At the time when "In this Verandah" was written Birney still believed that intelligence and shrewdness coupled with the life force — the coyote and the sun respectively — would outflank human prejudice and find the way to a better social order. More than that, he seems to see in the coyote something of a kindred spirit; the animal represents irreverence, wildness, and intellectual quickness pitted against authority. It is an animal that is quintessentially free, independent, and intelligent, and Birney's fondness for the beast may reflect his own changing attitude toward society. After the war he no longer wanted to be part of a society that he considered to be corrupt and destructive; he preferred to be like the coyote: an outsider and a pariah, in society's terms; he wanted to stay shrewdly clear of man and his dangerous follies while observing them from a safe distance.

Finally, there is Birney's use of tree and lake imagery to symbolize various aspects of the human condition. The tree is an especially evocative symbol since it represents living things gifted with the miraculous ability to renew themselves even when they seem to be dead, and it can be found throughout Birney's poetry from very early works like "On a Diary" to his latest poems like "the gray woods exploding" and "six for Ian." In "On a Diary" the green tree motif dominates the poem, representing the growth to maturity of a young woman poet from fifteen to twenty-five during the war years in England. The vicissitudes which she must face — loneliness, grief, deprivation, publishers' rejection slips — are nicely represented by the frosts and storms that threaten the growth of a young tree, but in the end she flourishes and triumphs. Birney makes similar use of the green tree image in *Trial of a City;* the Chief recalls that "In the green shooting of my chieftainship the Captain's cloudboat came" and Mrs. Anyone's triumphant rejection of Powers's cynicism is based upon the knowledge that "Because of the green bulb within us we leaf to joy." In "the gray woods exploding" Birney retains the tree as symbol of life but adapts its greenness to the dun-colored condition of the Australian landscape. The gray man explodes into an account of a colorful and fiery life just as the Australian forests burst into leaf or into flame with the coming of water or fire. And in his great love lyrics written in the 1970s Birney once again turns to the tree image to express his ideas about the cycle of life and death. In poems like "she is" Birney uses the tree as a complex metaphor for his awareness of his own old age, for the spiritual nourishment derived from his lover, and for the promise which he finds in the recurring cycles of the tree's existence:

> through the cold time
> she holds me
> with evergreen
> devotion
> she bears up my whiteness. . . .

Love, like the arboreal cycle, holds the promise of eternity.

Birney also recognizes that a lake can be symbolic of the beauty inherent in every living creature. Like man, a lake is capable of being polluted and corrupted by contact with human beings. Beyond that, there is the mystery inherent in water as the source of all life. The lake or pond, then, becomes a fertile source of images for Birney; he uses a muddy pond to represent the dark neurotic mind in "Introvert," a mountain lake to reflect the fears and incomprehension of the intrusive man in "Bushed." In "daybreak on lake opal: high rockies'' the lake symbolizes all that is pure, lovely, and unsullied in the world, and Birney's praise of that natural glory harks back to similar passages in "David," where the boys in some sense saw their own purity of purpose and love for the natural world mirrored in the pristine mountain lakes. Even in a light-hearted occasional poem like "in purdy's ameliasburg" the jocular reference to Roblin Lake as a "cosy girl's-belly-button" hints at Birney's delight in the pastoral innocence of the scene after spending the winter in Toronto. In contrast to these symbols of natural and youthful innocence there is the lake in "what's so big about GREEN?", raped and raddled like a skid-row prostitute. The aging and corruption of the lake are like the process of aging and corruption in a man too long exposed to the pressures and temptations of organized society.

III   *Birney and the Canadian Scene*

In a review of *David and Other Poems* John Sutherland said that Birney alone among the young generation of Canadian poets made consistent use of the Canadian landscape: " 'David' . . . brings the mountains so near that they hover and press upon the mind. . . . A poem like 'Hands' . . . gains a real beauty because it draws in factual details of a familiar landscape."[15] The same could be said of much of Birney's other work, especially of his early poems. In fact, although Birney contemptuously rejected "the first trillium on the hill" school of Canadian nature poets, much of his own very best nature poetry appeared early in his career when he was still either consciously or unconsciously working in the tradition of Canadian poets like Lampman and Roberts or, for that matter, Floris Clark McLaren, whose poems reflect the same type of sharp objective observation of the natural scene as one finds throughout "David" and elsewhere in Birney's poetry. This tradition of pure nature poetry is also reflected in "Poem," written before Birney became more engrossed in political and social questions. In fact, willy-nilly Birney's fame is likely to rest in good part upon his skill as an observer of the natural world; at the very heart of his oeuvre must lie "David," "Slug in Woods," "Poem" (or "Flying Fish"), "Aluroid," parts of *Trial of a City,* and so much more that depends for its power and beauty upon a brilliant evocation of the wilderness. Even in his subsequent poems, like "Page of Gaspé" and "North Star West," when he is simply writing about the country, the tone becomes lyrical and even loving as though he himself found peace and satisfaction in that tranquil landscape.

Yet, Birney the sun-worshiper and lover of life is also aware of the defects of living in Canada. In "Winter Saturday" the cocoon becomes a metaphor for man's existence in the Canadian winter; life is reduced to the rhythm of the chrysalis as a result of the numbness and sterility of the winter landscape. His evocation of the prairie summertime is not much more encouraging; "Prairie Counterpoint" is rife with the ennui of Saturday afternoon in a prairie town. In a larger sense, the prairie, the tundra, blizzards and cold, those hostile lonely elements, may be construed as Birney's metaphors for the barrenness and sterility of Canadian society, and this in turn may partially account for his wandering in search of the warmth of the sun, the intellectual and physical challenge of the mountains, and the fecundity of the sea.

In much of his early poetry and in almost all of his later work, of course, Birney uses the interaction of man and nature to illustrate some social or political comment. "Ellesmereland," written when Birney was beginning to have serious doubts about the future of the human race, implies that nature is no longer only indifferent but has become actively hostile to the existence of man; once man has destroyed himself nature will not make the mistake of creating him again. The same sense of patient hostility to mankind is expressed in "Sixth Grade Biology Quiz" and "tongareva atoll"; nature is quietly waiting for man to finish with his wars, as represented by the Liberator's crew, and his vanities, suggested by the haircombs and duraluminum stars, and go away. The last three lines of "tongareva atoll" —

> The oysters as usual say nothing
>
> They're waiting for the night
> the great pearl in the skyshell falls

— hint at Birney's characteristic conviction that some natural disaster will accomplish man's end if he does not destroy himself first. This whole sense of man as a temporary aberration on the part of nature was expressed in Birney's work as early as 1928, when he composed "Grey-Rocks," and has persisted throughout his poetry, emerging eventually in images of man as a disease in the body of nature in poems like "Transcontinental."

Margaret Atwood has suggested that a writer's attitude toward nature will to some extent reflect his attitude toward sexuality.[16] In Birney's case this contention does seem to hold true. Birney's conception of nature as indifferent to man and his folly is reflected in some of his poems involving women. "The Ballad of Mr. Chubb," "Twenty-third Flight," "Appeal to a Lady with a Diaper," and *Trial of a City* all deal with women who are superior to and rather indifferent to the hurrying, aging, futile men. Lena in "The Ballad of Mr. Chubb" is as dangerous as any force in nature, and as untrustworthy; she is a human counterpart to "the Greenland lodger," "that madcap virgin mother of ice" in "the mammoth corridors" who waits patiently to sweep man's puny contrivings before her.

On the other hand, Birney has a profound sense of nature as a source of solace to man. After trying naively to alter the course of history during a wretched summer in a stinking city, Gordon Saunders is partly brought to his senses and finds solace in Matthew Arnold's *Lines Written in Kensington Gardens*. He comes to realize that he can achieve very little with fickle and selfish human beings but that he might find peace and stability in an alignment with the natural world. This view is counterbalanced by poems like "Climbers" and "David." The former is an expression of the futility of man's attempts to dissociate himself from his own kind; he can appreciate nature's beauties but in the end must return to live in the world of men. Bob, too, in "David" is awakened to the fact that association with nature can bring pain as well as knowledge; in this poem nature is cruel only to her own: to the live pine, the robin, the mountain goat, and to David himself, who is very close to being a creature of the wild. In the end, however, Birney remains confident that nature will still comfort him in her embrace if only he can be alone with her. In "sunday nightfall in Winnipeg," after observing the filth, rudeness, and degeneracy of the city of man Birney is struck by the image of his old friend the sun reflected in a dirty window and is comforted by the sight of it in "the beautiful antediluvian sky."

CHAPTER 6

Poetic Technique

O NE of the arguments that Birney has urged throughout most of his adult life is that poetry and prose writing are techniques that can be taught; in the face of heavy opposition from university faculties he pointed to the long list of major writers who have benefited from creative-writing courses or who have given such courses themselves. To Birney the practice of writing and revising is a fundamental exercise even when the author knows there is little hope of his work being published, and the exercise is all the more effective when it is conducted under the guidance of an experienced author.[1] Birney also states categorically that many of his poems were initially five-finger exercises undertaken to help him master a certain verse form or metrical pattern.[2]

The belief that writing is a craft to be learned, combined with the habit of practicing new forms, has led Birney to master a multitude of poetic techniques ranging from Anglo-Saxon alliterative verse to concrete and found poetry. As an undergraduate, the contemporary poets he admired most were Hardy, Housman, de la Mare, Eliot, and Jeffers.[3] He also pays tribute to Chaucer's craftsmanship, his "rhythmic grace and poised nuance of phrase," and recognized that he was the "greatest of all English humourists."[4] From these traditional beginnings he has moved on to adapt James Joyce's wordplay, American jazz rhythms, and the theories of Ezra Pound and the Black Mountain poets to his own purposes.

Another aspect of Birney's interest in technique is manifested in the fact that he deplores the Canadian writers' tendency to let themselves be categorized as "poet," "novelist," or "journalist" without being able to break out of the stereotype and become all-round "men of letters," or, as Birney prefers to call them, "men of images" as Hardy, Dickens, Stephen Crane, and others were.[5] To Birney, this compartmentalization of Canadian writers is largely their own fault: "Layton and Purdy live content in the valley that Carman and Pratt settled, MacLennan and Callaghan in the next. The critics, on Black Mountain, watch both ways against cattle raids."[6] Birney himself has always striven to be as versatile and to command as many literary genres as he could; as a result, his oeuvre includes two novels, a great deal of poetry, half a dozen short stories, stage and radio plays, radio and print journalism, and a large and catholic body of literary criticism. Moreover, Birney has a penchant for tinkering with a work until he has transposed it from one genre to another; the first editor to print "Joe Harris" set it up as a poem, the second as a short story; then a composer, Lorne Betts, set it to music as the libretto for a male chorus and orchestra.[7]

Nor has Birney agreed to decline into a moribund old age, resting upon his laurels and ceasing to experiment further; he has continued to learn, to revise, and to produce new work. As George Woodcock said in a review of *Selected Poems,* Birney is not the sort of poet who willingly indicates that the days of his best works are past; "...the sense that the future is always open, that nothing written is ever quite finished while its author is still alive, is one of Birney's special characteristics as a writer...." Woodcock also claims that this characteristic was the basis of Birney's friendship with "that arch-reviser" Malcolm Lowry.[8] Al Purdy has compared him to "the French painter, Pierre Bonnard, in his old age sneaking into the Louvre with paint brushes under his coat ... to retouch and alter his own paintings hung on the sacred walls."[9]

One can follow the track of Birney's revisions and corrections throughout his work. When he realized that the kites to which he referred in "David" were actually hawks he had to rework the last part of the stanza in which the reference occurs in order to maintain the meter and the assonantal rhyme pattern. "Remarks for the Part of Death" from *Now Is Time* was recast as "Remarks Decoded from Outer Space" in *Selected Poems.* "The Road to Nijmegen" was completely revised before it was republished in *Selected Poems,* and some of the line lengths were altered before it next appeared in *The Poems of Earle Birney.* "Smalltown Hotel" was totally refurbished for its inclusion in *Selected Poems,* as was "Anglosaxon Street," from which one entire stanza was dropped. The list is endless and it continues to grow as Birney's work is republished, but the changes in the poems are more than just the result of a careful craftsman polishing his wares. They reflect Birney's absorption of new poetic techniques from younger writers and his willingness to apply them to his own work.

I *Alliterative Verse*

One of the by-products of Birney's long study of Anglo-Saxon verse is his profound familiarity with the alliterative verse form, a familiarity that allowed him to adapt the form to his own ends. He does not share Chaucer's contempt for poetry that goes "rum-raf-rum by letter" but freely uses it wherever he thinks it may serve his purpose. In the 1950s and 1960s he was much interested in the prosody of the Beats and the Black Mountain poets, especially in their use of the line length adapted to the breathing rhythm of the reader, but in fact he already had a solid knowledge of the principle underlying this technique since the caesura or breathing space is a standard component of Anglo-Saxon alliterative verse. From his early imitations of classic alliterative verse he moved on to poems like "once high upon a hill," where there are two or three breathing spaces or pauses per line in lieu of punctuation, a device which renders the poem subtle, free-moving, and uncluttered. Birney also moved from the classic use of the exclamatory "O!" at the beginning of the line for heroic effect to the point where he used it either for heroic or mock-heroic effect. In "Anglosaxon Street," for example, he subtly distorted the heroic exclamation into a bestial grunt, "Hoy," emphasizing the banality of working-class life, while in "Pachucan Miners" the clear, traditional "O" reinforces the legendary motif of the poem. In fact, Birney even adapted the classic "O!" for use in his later love poetry so that in poems like "she is" it forms part of the poet's fervent expression of adoration.

Although there are such bits and pieces of the alliterative tradition scattered throughout the Birney canon, the best example of a sustained use of the technique is "Anglosaxon Street," in which one finds the classic consonantal links between the on-stave and the off-stave, the caesura dividing the staves, and the use of the kenning. "Mappemounde" is almost as perfect from a technical point of view, but is, of course, much shorter and rather more difficult for the average reader to understand than is the satirical "Anglo-saxon Street." Here again one finds the alliterative links, including some double alliteration: "Adread in that mere we drift to map's end," and the kennings: "bale-twisters," "gleewords," and, as Birney himself points out, the characteristic speech rhythms of the

English language, so that each half-line tends to have "a heavy primary, a lighter but still definite secondary and an unaccented syllable."[10] But perhaps the most subtle effects of the poem derive from the fact that Birney has combined the Norse or Anglo-Saxon meter and language with the Italianate sonnet length. As a result, the reader is deftly led through a familiar verse form to the mysterious and frightening allusions with which Birney seeks to illuminate the dark corners of the human heart.

"Takkakaw Falls" is a case in which Birney has departed from the Anglo-Saxon line but has retained the booming speech rhythms — "Júpiter, Thór, how he thúnders!" — of the heroic verse and combined it with a very complex use of alliteration and with allusions to the Norse gods to suggest that Takkakaw is also a river god. In this poem the alliteration is sometimes used within a single line — "vaulting a valley" — but it is also used in a more extended pattern so that it not only links up the various lines but helps to underscore the physical shape of the poem itself:

> *f*alls
> *f*alls gyring, *f*lings
> rain rainbows like peacock *f*lights....

In these lines the reader is reminded that the poem deals with both a waterfall and a tragic "fall" at the same time that the layout of the lines on the page helps to suggest the shape of a waterfall. Further on in the poem, as the river flattens out in bottomlands near the sea, the lines also lengthen and "flatten out" both physically and acoustically before rising once again to batter their way toward the heavens in powerful staccato steps.

In his early poetry, at least, Birney often employed alliterative verse to indicate the seriousness of his theme. He uses it in "War Winters" to express his awed misgivings about the war; the somber music of the lines befits his insight into the winter of the human heart. In "Conrad Kain" he uses it to underscore the essential purity of motive and the heroism of his protagonist. In *Trial of a City* it is used to indicate that the speaker, either Professor E. O. Seen or William Langland, is in possession of irrefutable and damning facts; the stern old speech patterns suggest a judgment based upon a tradition as old as time and infinitely more enduring than Legion's hysterical pleading. In the case of "David," in which the meter is based upon the meter of Archibald MacLeish's *Conquista-*

dor, and, farther back, upon the eleventh-century *Chanson de Roland,* which Birney had read in the original while at Berkeley,[11] Birney uses assonance rather than consonance to achieve an alliterative effect, but here again the round, booming vowel sounds introduce a solemn note of foreboding: "...I remember only / The long ascent of the lonely valley...." The immediacy with which Birney's images evoke the beauty of summer and youth in the Rockies is underscored with the archetypal knowledge that "Ever at the latter end of joy comes woe."

II *Lyric Poetry*

After mentioning that Birney's mother had committed him "until far into his teens to play the organ at church services," Peter Noel-Bentley goes on to say that Birney's early musical training has resulted in the fact that Birney's metaphors "include an enormous number of musical terms and images. And his poems themselves reveal a deep awareness of the importance of sound and voice in conveying the poetic vision or idea."[12] Perhaps the outstanding example of Birney's command of "sound and voice" is "to swindon from london by britrail aloud / bagatelle." Although the title suggests that the poem is a mere exercise and of little importance, in fact it is one of Birney's most perfectly worked out tone poems. No one who has ever traveled by British Rail can fail to experience once again all the sensations of such a trip as he reads this poem; the departing whistle, the slow exit from the station, the train bumping over the switches in the railway yard and then picking up speed until it rocks steadily along, flashing past the green fields and through the streaming rain, occasionally whistling for a crossing — "B O O oooooottt! Boot!" — until it slows and squeals to a halt, are all vividly evoked.

"Bangkok Boy" is another example of Birney's technical virtuosity. The meter of the lines referring to the boy is lively, syncopated, fired by a series of explosive "p" and "t" sounds and linked by a series of strong internal rhymes. Then, as the poem shifts its focus to the Western tourists the rhythm slows; the long vowel sounds suggest the lassitude and boredom engendered by the heat of the tropics; the meter of "girlies / imported to strip to the beat of copulation" suggests the lewd wailing music of the strip joint, and when Birney reflects in the second-last stanza upon the unpleasant fate awaiting the Bangkok boy here too the rhythm becomes slow, ponderous, and pensive before shifting one last time into the short, jazzy syllables that mimic the actions of the lively dancing boy. Each of the two contrasting elements in the poem — the boy and the tourists — has its own clearly defined "signature" or melody; the boy's is based upon a staccato, syncopated, assonantal rhythm that gives way to a slower, almost journalistic, line recounting the sordid facts of adult lives. This alternating long and short line pattern of "Bangkok Boy" is reminiscent of Birney's use of long and short stanzas in the original version of "Anglosaxon Street." The latter poem opened with two eight-line stanzas, then a five-line stanza, three four-line stanzas, and two three-line stanzas as the rhythm of life on the street picked up, before dropping back to a penultimate five-liner as the slum drifted off to sleep in the evening.

Similar examples of Birney's use of rhythm to reinforce theme can be found in poems like "Honolulu" and "Quebec May" and even in a short story like "Enigma in Ebony." The greatest part of "Honolulu" is set in a hurrying, frantic meter suited to the frantic yammering of the American boor preoccupied with food, money, and sex, but it shifts abruptly in the last four lines into a cool, slow meter to express the child's tranquil contemplation of the natural world. Birney does something similar in "Enigma in Ebony" at the point midway through the story where, after taking the professor on a hair-rising ride to the look-out, the driver decides to proceed at a smooth, orderly pace. The jumbled descriptions and jerky sentences of the first scene give way to calm, lingering, detailed observations of the town and its people. In "Quebec May" Birney is stimulated to write in a racing meter by the rushing exuberance of spring; the dominant note is struck by the sibilant "s" and "sh" sounds that occur in nearly every line, simulating the rushing of the thaw-swollen creek, and the lively four-beat line evokes the stomp and squeal of a Québecois jig danced at a sugar party.

Many examples of this technique can be found in *The Damnation of Vancouver;* perhaps one of the best is the use of ballad meter for the speeches of Mrs. Anyone:

> Two flickers knocked on a cedar's door
> Three finches ran fugues in the wind
> And the scent of the primula moved in my world
> However my world had sinned.

Because of its connotations of common parlance, tradition, and a cultural heritage, the ballad meter suggests that the woman is speaking of something enduring, of interest to rich and poor alike. It also soothes and comforts the ear after Legion's jingling Gilbert and Sullivan rhyme —

> Really, Mr. President,
>   This seems to me irregular.
> I don't know what you're pulling,
>   But I hope it's not our leg you are

— and Powers's nonstop doubletalk.

An even more subtle instance of Birney's use of rhythm to reinforce theme occurs in "Francisco Tresguerras." Here Birney ironically employs the same meter as Browning used in "The Lost Leader"; as a result the poem suggests that the citizens of Celaya once had an artistic leader who is now lost to them by their own choice. As for Tresguerras, he finds himself in the artist's heaven, which is also his hell; that is to say he is in the position of still being able to question mankind's tastes and values even when he himself is dead and no longer able to create.

It is not possible to leave the subject of Birney's use of meter to support theme without at least a brief consideration of "Answers to a Grade-School Biology Test," "Oldster," and "Transistor." In the first of these poems the singsong meter suggests the rote learning that Birney detests, while the contrapuntal layout of the lines, combined with that meter, contains a hint of ecclesiastical chant with its overtones of death and damnation. The second poem, "Oldster," has a curious internal rhyme scheme: pairs of rhyming words are closely linked in every second line. The effect of these little explosions of rhyme — "green sheen," "black crack," "gale's flail" — set into each two lines of slow-moving vowel sounds, is to suggest flickers of life still spurting through the old tree as it dreams and drowses toward death. To appreciate this flickering metrical pattern one may contrast it with the smooth, flowing lines of "Transistor," where the long and short "o" sounds combine to evoke the timeless crooning sound of lullaby or ballad:

> She paused only once   to down a glass
> the engineer poured from the rum he'd brought

He knew what songs to ask for
and out they came now whorling
as if her voice were immortal and separate
within her....

The former poem deals with the fact that time must have a stop
while the latter conjures up a magic whereby time may go on
forever.

III   *Rhyme*

Birney's use of rhyme is as interesting as is his use of meter.
Although the great majority of his work is written in free verse, his
poetry is remarkable for the amount of near-rhyme he employs.
The first and greatest example of sustained use of near-rhyme in
Birney's poetry, of course, is "David," with its carefully worked
out pattern of rhymes and near-rhymes within each line,[13] but Birney's fondness for near-rhyme is manifested throughout his work.
The virtues of this technique are that it permits great flexibility of
language and avoids the rigid end-stopping effect of true rhyme;
moreover, for a poet writing in the English language it offers the
further benefit of freeing him from the forced diction that inevitably results from the notorious lack of rhyming words in English.
Characteristically, Birney will use a combination of rhyme and
near-rhyme in the same poem; from this combination he derives a
desirable linking effect without distracting the reader from the
voice of the speaker in the poem. "For Steve" is a good example of
the technique; the calm, discursive tone of the poem is allowed to
move forward without impediment because of the avoidance of a
rigid use of rhyme. Still, the poem is written in the Spenserian
stanza and Birney uses rhyming words at the ends of lines wherever
he can do so without interrupting the flow of thought. The result is
a pleasing informality of tone without the loss of structural regular-
ity. The same thing is true of "The Bear on the Delhi Road," in
which a considerable number of lines actually do rhyme, but in the
most natural and unforced manner. Wherever the rhyme pattern
threatens to become intrusive or artificial, Birney reverts to near-
rhyme or blank verse.

Something similar can be seen in poems like "Dusk on the Bay,"
"Prairie Counterpoint," and "Poem." Most of the lines in "Dusk
on the Bay" are linked by near end-rhymes: "fall" and "calling,"

"row" and "yellows," "guns," "sun," and "smudged"; but the rhymes do not occur in any predictable pattern, with the result that the coherence of the poem is established in the most unobtrusive fashion while leaving the reader free to concentrate on its theme and its imagery. On the other hand, in a poem like "Prairie Counterpoint," where stanzas of monologue alternate with stanzas of description of the natural world, Birney sets the monologue in unrhymed blank verse while the descriptive stanzas are set in a regular rhymed pattern, abc abc, def def, and so on. The effect of the blank verse, combined with the speaker's words, is to suggest the transience of human concerns, while the regularly rhymed stanzas evoke the perpetual cycles of the natural world. "Poem" is a case where Birney's preference for lines ending in near-rhymes is combined with strong internal rhymes within each line. The result is a nervous, spurting rhythm — "stall and fall and soar and then" — that depicts the manner in which the flying fish burst frantically from the water ahead of their pursuer.

IV   *Imagery*

Birney's use of imagery is as carefully coordinated with his themes as is his use of rhyme. "David" and "Climbers" are outstanding examples not only of his ability to depict the glorious scenery of the Rocky Mountains but also of his technique of coordinating the images with the theme of the poem. "Climbers" in a sense is a miniature version of "David"; the images in both poems begin on a rising note of excitement as the climbers quit their workaday world and move upward toward the beauty and challenge of the mountains; both poems pause to describe the glories of the alpine scenery before going on to the pleasures derived from conquering the peaks and the sensation of being alone in the wilderness; then, each poem, to a greater or lesser degree, abruptly pulls its protagonists back into the world of men. In both cases these effects derive from Birney's use of imagery. The "squeak-squeal of wheels" and "the stench of the highest backlot" in "Climbers" parallels "the snoring under fetid tents" of "David"; both poems have central sections full of vivid pictures of the mountains, and both end with an evocation of nature's indifference. "The pointless point of the peak" in "Climbers" echoes the tone of the last stanza of "David" with its reference to "the incurious clouds" remaining as the only witnesses to Bob's travail.

For sheer imagist power, however, the best of Birney's poems are probably "Pachucan Miners," "State of Sonora," "Introvert," and "Caribbean Kingdoms." In the first of these Birney's brilliant use of black and silver imagery not only evokes the portrait of a silver-mining town but reinforces the mythological and historical motifs, the themes of men searching backward into myth and history for a knowledge of their own origins. Moreover, the same theme is sustained and developed by the vertical imagery in the poem; all motion on the part of the men is upward or downward. The miners rise from the darkness of the mine into the darkness of the evening; initially, everything that is silver is forbidden them: they are below the "white Olympus of the gringos," the gate to the silver mine is guarded. But then as they descend into their own town and into their own heritage silvery things — tequila, Eurydice's crucifix — become available to them as a matter of birthright and they themselves are transformed from a "defeated army" into "silver men."

Occasionally the vividness of Birney's imagery overpowers his theme, as is the case in "Introvert." Here Birney's imagery is so accurate that the poem actually recreates St. James's Park for the reader, and the park, as it turns out, is infinitely more beautiful and far more interesting than the introvert's mind.

Two examples of better controlled and therefore much more successful imagist poems are "State of Sonora" and "Caribbean Kingdoms." In the former, every harsh, clattering consonant evokes the dry, sunbaked state:

> Thin country with bright hard
> hide   Rain ricochets from adamantine
> ranges where wild peccaries
> scrabble   and clatters
> intact down baked
> ravines....

Even the references to La Palma and El Oasis are ironically set in the midst of descriptions of what those towns are really like — dusty, hot, and parched — and the references to the ocean are similarly unrelieved by any hope of coolness or refreshment. The day goes "sizzling" into the ocean, the islands in the Sea of Cortez are "guano-glazed," the fishermen are "gnarled as turtles." There is no need to visit Sonora; it is vividly present in Birney's poem.

The harsh brilliance of "State of Sonora" provides a perfect contrast to "Carribean Kingdoms," one of Birney's pictorially most beautiful poems and one of his most rhythmic. The vivid tropical imagery, the tranquil Wordsworthian contemplation of nature with its promise of peace after the animal world has ceased from troubling, and the carefully structured rhythms and rhyme patterns all serve to create an intense sense of peace, timelessness, and repose. In a sense, this poem, like "Slug in Woods," another nature poem of brilliant imagery, is something of a confession of faith; it is remarkable that Birney's most vivid imagery is not expended upon questions of war or poverty, but upon the tranquil cycles of the natural world.

V *Symmetry*

Another aspect of Birney's work which may or may not derive from his early musical training is his love of symmetry. *Down the Long Table,* for example, is perfectly symmetrical, with a structure that pivots around the freight-train episodes. Birney has said that he "tried to arrange a sequence of techniques from section one to 18; 18-19-20 are a pivot, and the book then repeats the techniques in a reverse order to get an over-all double spectrum...."[14] Similarly, the critic's complaint about the improbable reappearances of certain characters in *Turvey,* notably Mac and the SPO,[15] derives from a failure to understand Birney's love of balance and symmetry.   •

One of the best examples of this element in Birney's poetry is "Dusk on the Bay," with its symmetrical ordering of images toward and away from a center point for the purpose of ironic commentary. The early images of peace and beauty are played back in the second half of the poem in a horrifying and depressing context. The references to death and dismemberment in the first half of the poem are rendered inoppressive because they are clearly a function of a peaceful late afternoon at the beach: distance "unsexes" the bathers' legs and twilight makes them look as though their arms have been severed, whereas in the second half of the poem the limbs really have been "unsexed and severed," the drowning sailors really have been quenched. The impact of the poem derives from the fact that the placid lyricism, the commonplaces, of the first half of the poem are repeated in the second half in the light of a fierce apocalyptic vision; the same images serve both points of view with devastating effect.

This symmetrical ordering of images in Birney's poetry —

"Appeal to a Lady with a Diaper" is another case in point — is almost so common as to be endemic. The nine sections into which "David" is divided pivot about Section VI, the high point of the poem and the section in which the boys reach their zenith of youth, strength, success, and peace of mind. Up to that point everything in the poem contributes to a sense of upward progress toward knowledge; after that point every element combines in an inexorable movement toward disaster. In "Captain Cook" the images of the first three lines are reiterated in the last three both for ironic contrast and to lend cohesiveness to the poem. Birney does something similar in "Vitus Bering," where the opening lines are repeated at the end of the poem, thereby underlining the uses to which Bering's heroic sacrifice was put. In "Wake Island," on the other hand, the whole poem is an expansion of the basic stanzaic pattern of two long lines enclosing two shorter, rhyming lines in the sense that the imagery of the first and last stanzas — imagery of long journeys through cold and darkness — encloses the imagery of immediate human concerns — coffee, love, postcards, and scenery — in the four central stanzas. Here as elsewhere in Birney's work the overall effect is one of patient craftsmanship camouflaged by a bantering or irreverent tone.

VI *Experimental Verse*

Much of Birney's poetry is "experimental" in the sense that he will write in a certain form in order to master that form and add it to his repertoire: hence his work includes not only easily recognized sonnets, haiku, sestinas, villanelles, and ballads, but also more esoteric types of poetry such as aubades, chants, compleynts, and *chansons pieux*. Nevertheless, it has been said that Birney is seldom an innovator in poetic technique, preferring to borrow techniques from other writers whose work interests him.[16] It has also been suggested that he actually shrinks from the more outlandish forms of experimental verse, especially in the realm of typographical experimentation, but that for that very reason he forces himself to try his hand at it.[17] Certainly, at the beginning of his career as a poet he had nothing but harsh words for the obscure and the avant garde. As late as 1953 he wrote in the preface to his anthology of Canadian poetry, "...this collection has sought to avoid fashionably obscure or highly experimental work which, however 'great' it may eventually turn out to be, can offer at the moment little of the food of the imagination except to the very sophisticated palate."[18]

Despite this, Birney's career has been a long succession of experiments, and perhaps the earliest of these were his forays into the realm of Joycean wordplay. Like Joyce, Birney seems to be inspired by chance associations of events and people and by the fact that odd combinations of sounds can serve to suggest a meaning better than can formal words and phrases. "Mammorial Stunzas for Aimee Simple McFarcin" is his first important poem in this area; the punning, distorted language is used as an irreverent contrast to the overwrought piety of the evangelist.

Birney also made extensive use of the Joycean technique in *Trial of a City,* upon which Northrop Frye commented, ". . . for virtuosity of language there has never been anything like it in Canadian poetry."[19] In fact, the Joycean foolery — "there's no one present from the Future," "The V-Dayls of the dooming, Mr. Legion, are not yet warred out foully" — provides a framework for the poignant lyricism of the Salish chief, for Gassy Jack's hearty lecherousness, and for Langland and E. O. Seen's scholarly reserve. The Future, in the person of Gabriel Powers, can afford to be lighthearted because he knows everything and is responsible for nothing. His irreverent wit also makes a nice contrast with Legion's frantic pleading and supercilious clichés. Also, the Joycean double-talk has the advantage of being well suited to represent the language of the future. Anthony Burgess and various science-fiction writers have tried to invent such a language, but none of their attempts is so felicitous as Birney's use of Joycean near-English. As the Minister of History observes, "Mr. Powers has been briefed by the Office of the Future and must use its language. It's not his fault if English has changed again."

Birney has also admitted attempting to master "the breath-accent and the heart-beat of a Black Mountain line series."[20] This would seem to imply that he was influenced to some extent by Kenneth Rexroth's interest in Oriental or foreign poets, and by William Carlos Williams's use of vernacular speech and vivid observation, especially of sensory experience. Yet, the whole question of the amount of influence exercised upon Birney by the Black Mountain poets is obscure. For example, the "projective verse" of the Black Mountain school was neither didactic nor necessarily designed for the entertainment of an audience; it was supposed to reflect a poetic experience and to underline the Black Mountain school's belief in the identity of form and content. Instead of writing for an audience the Black Mountain poets were writing for themselves, and if the reader did not understand them he was supposed to study and adapt his thinking until he did.[21] Little or none of this attitude appears in Birney's poetry. He is very much involved in communicating with people, and in his poetry his awareness of his audience is paramount; although he may appear to be the lonely observer of man and nature he is intensely interested in broadcasting his observations as widely as possible. In the whole body of his work, with a few unfortunate exceptions such as his use of the word "aluroid" for the title of a poem about a cat and some of his more tortured exercises in concrete, there is very little that is solipsistic or obscure.[22]

What can be said about the connection between Birney's work and that of the Black Mountain poets is that the *Black Mountain Review* was published from 1954 to 1957, that is to say at a time when Birney was, as always, receptive to the stimulus of new ideas. About this time the Beat poets were also making themselves heard and doing for poetry what Lenny Bruce was doing for the Free Speech movement: they were liberating ancient Anglo-Saxon four-letter words from the restraints of North American puritanism.[23] As for the Black Mountain poets, although they rejected the total formlessness of free verse and Beat poetry, they did develop a line based upon the rhythm of the heartbeat and the natural breathing pattern of the reader which "led them to rather short-line poems, containing only one strong stress, [which] created an agreeable effect of space, simple intensity, and delicate patterning on the page."[24]

Some of Birney's earliest experiments in the use of typography to reinforce theme include "Memory No Servant," "Letter to a Cuzco Priest," and "Way to the West." In "Memory No Servant" the first fourteen lines are an idle reverie about the half-forgotten details of a holiday in Mexico, and the lines run smoothly and regularly down the left-hand margin to the point where a painful fact intrudes into the idyll. Birney's vivid recollection of a turtle crushed by his car is set off from the rest of the poem, and the most painful detail of all — the fact that the turtle's head was still moving — is emphasized in a single agonized word set all by itself at the end of the poem. In "Letter to a Cuzco Priest" Birney employs offset lines partly to differentiate between direct address and narrative and partly to emphasize the emotional intensity of his words to the priest. The calm, ironic recitation of the facts leading up to the slaughter of the Indians by the army is counterpointed by the whispered, confessional intensity of Birney's words to the priest — "Father forgive yourself," "Father worship yourself," "Father you were not with those shepherds" — while the staggered typography of the poem underlies the shifts in tone and mood. In "Way to the West" as in "billboards build freedom of choice" Birney uses both offset lines and capital letters for special effects; the former signals shifts from observation of the pandemonium that is Sudbury to the poet's reflection upon the effect that those phenomena are having upon himself, while the latter are used to suggest the bombastic effect of the area's billboards, set, as they are, along the road to hell.

In the early 1960s Birney began to pay attention to the "concrete poetry" school, an apparently serious movement flourishing in Europe and South America whose chief Canadian practitioners at that time were bp nichol and Bill Bissett. The concrete poets generally divided their work into "clean" and "dirty" categories. In clean concrete the visual shape of the poem is dominant while its syntactic meaning is secondary, while dirty concrete, the less effective of the two according to its devotees, is characterized by both physical shapelessness and obscure convolutions of the linguistic elements: "In dirty concrete there can be no immediate response to the whole, only cumulative interpretation gained by painstaking labour."[25] An example of clean concrete in Birney's work is "for esther"; the shape of the poem is paramount while the syntactic meaning, if there is one, is largely a matter of the reader's imagination. On the other hand, "up her can nada" probably fits into the category of dirty concrete.

bp nichol has said that

"concrete" or "experimental" poetry concerns itself with a return to the simpler elements of language. For Birney this has meant a return to the ear, and a search for some way to orchestrate for it.... early things like "shetland grandaunt" show an awareness of dialectic, of accent. and the accent is the key here. enhancement. he wants to show the rise and fall of the human voice so he lets the line rise and fall.[26]

In other early experiments with concrete, Birney set the last word in "Epidaurus" vertically to suggest the path of a falling pin; later he was to shape the entire last stanza into the parabolic path of a bomb. The dates of composition attributed to his series of poems called "buildings" (1947/1957) suggest that he was actually experimenting with concrete poetry well before he came under the influence even of its young Canadian practitioners like Bissett and nichol, and "Appeal to a Lady with a Diaper," first published in 1957, has lines that go jouncing across the page to suggest a swaying, bouncing bus ride.

The inherent weakness of the theories of the Black Mountain poets and the concrete poets has been described as

the danger of a certain confusion between visual or spatial arrangements on the one hand and movement of the poem in time on the other. If there is a significant formal weakness in the method of Charles Olson and Robert Duncan, it shows up precisely in this confusion. The avowed intention to "get on with it, keep moving," is blocked by a certain narcissism of form, the poet's over-absorption in his own voice not as the embodying element of the curve of the poem but as a reflection of his own self-awareness.[27]

This is very true of some of Birney's poems, like "there are delicacies." This poem's original stanzaic form was reshaped to resemble the mechanism of a watch when it was reprinted in *what's so big about GREEN?* Unfortunately, in the concrete version the reader must spend so much time sorting out the syntax that the impact of the poem is lost. The delicacies of feeling and expression become obscure and cluttered and the reader becomes bored and frustrated by the contrived "concrete" layout of the second version.

Much the same thing is true of poems like "Nayarít" and the "buildings" group, which are some of Birney's less successful attempts at concrete poetry. In "Nayarít" an otherwise simple and effective lyric is lost in the maze of typographical distortions; the reader is so busy unraveling these distortions that he tends to forget to follow the theme of the poem. The four poems in the "buildings" series are essentially bits of whimsy: "buildings are made in squares for steepling / buildings are made in curves for peopling." In this particular case the first line is set in the form of a square steeple and the second in the curving form of a woman's breasts, but in all of these poems the element of fun is overwhelmed by the labor required to unscramble the poem from its concrete form.

On the other hand, some of Birney's poetry has benefited from being reset as concrete. "still" or "like an eddy" is a chant; hence the early versions had the same words repeated in different orders in successive lines and the former poem began and ended with the word "still." Birney has one concrete version shaped like an eddy and one printed in such a way that it can be cut out and pasted to the leaves of a mobile. One of the most successful of all his concrete poems is "alaska passage." The shape of the poem suggests a steamer nosing its way through the passage while the forest-clad slopes march downward to the sea, and the first line, ending "...alaska passage alas," evokes a note of lingering regret over the invasion and destruction of another wild free region by man. "up her can nada" would be a more or less meaningless collection of puns and phrases were it not for the fact that these elements adorn a crude map of upper Canada and derive a witty aptness from their positions on that map.

Finally, there is the matter of Birney's experiments with pop poetry. Ralph Hicklin has said that "the raw experience of pop poetry ... is anything that is verbal and common: billboards, commercials, labels. These commonplaces the poet can manipulate to make them into a satire of themselves, or into a poetic record of the time."[28] The pop poetry movement, in fact, is an analog of the Pop Art movement of the late 1950s, a movement that was led by artists like Andy Warhol and that featured the artistic reproduction of common artifacts of twentieth-century industrial society: soup cans, hamburgers, Brillo pads, and the like. In Birney's case, the most important manifestations of pop poetry are his jukollages, although he has also created one computer poem, used some campus theater steps for poetic effect, and written, or drawn, some amusing "pnomes": calendar poems in which the days and dates are accurate but the names of the days and months are oddball distortions of familiar words.

Birney's jukollages are in the tradition of found poetry, i.e., poetic passages which are already in existence and which only require the poet or artist to discover them and draw the attention of the public to them; there is no act of creation in the traditional sense of a controlled shaping of words or material.[29] Thus his "found swahili serenade" is an arrangement of popular song titles taken from a jukebox. The words may be bitter, sarcastic, or openly prurient but that is more or less a matter of chance; Birney could rearrange the order of the titles to achieve some of this effect but ultimately he was constrained by the ordering of the words within the titles themselves, so that the poem is really an artifact, a memento of one part of the civilization of the twentieth century.

Birney has acknowledged the effect of the electronic media, especially radio and the tape recorder, with its playback capability, upon the current generation of poets; the result has been to make them move from dense, convoluted poetic expressions toward the popular realm of folksinging,[30] and there is something of this in Birney's poems like "Moon down Elphinstone" which is essentially a ballad. He has also said that "the future is with the disc, tape, film, even more than with the printed book...."[31] But for all that it can fairly be said that much of Birney's experimental poetry — the mobiles, the alphabirneys, the concrete — was merely a stage in his development as a poet and that he has left that stage permanently behind. From his experiments with poetic forms he kept the best and most important elements, namely the absence of capitalization, the breathing space in place of punctuation, and the occasional variation in type face and size and the practice of shaping some poems for added visual impact. The result is a poetry of great power and suppleness, a line that lies cleanly on the page, and a thought pattern that can be followed easily, uninhibited by conventional marks of punctuation.

VII *Narrative Poems*

Birney has been judged to be "the only rival of Pratt as the creator of heroic narrative on a bold scale and, unlike Pratt, he has been consistently experimental."[32] He himself says that when he began writing poetry around 1940 he was in active revolt against the pedantry and obscurity of poets like Auden and Eliot and that he wanted to return to a narrative poetry characterized by clear-cut imagery.[33] In the ensuing years he has written a series of narrative poems including "David," the speeches of the Salish chief and Gassy Jack in *The Damnation of Vancouver,* "The Ballad of Kootenay Brown," and "Moon Down Elphinstone" that illuminate and preserve a series of now-vanished aspects of Canadian life, and others like "the gray woods exploding" and "Four Feet Between" that recount funny or tragic mementos of Birney's experiences in various parts of the world.

The tragic element in Birney's narrative poems, of course, is omnipresent. Even a rather whimsical poem like "Four Feet Between" has an undertone of regret at the difficulties of trying to communicate with another person, just as "cucarachas in fiji," for all its lighthearted banter, reflects upon the relative impermanence of mankind. "Conrad Kain" is perhaps Birney's only truly optimistic narrative poem and that is because it recounts the life of a man who was almost totally divorced from the concerns of the world, as though Kain's disregard for getting and spending, his disinterest in politics, and his absolute devotion to his craft as a mountain climber preserved him intact from the wrath of the gods. All of Birney's other narrative poems tend to end in tragedy, as in "David" or "Moon Down Elphinstone," or else they strike a note of sadness for a way of life that has passed, as in the speeches of the Salish chief and Gassy Jack, or for youth and beauty that have been destroyed by time, as in "the gray woods exploding" and "The Ballad of Kootenay Brown."

"David" is by any standard Birney's finest narrative poem; in fact it has been acclaimed as "the best poem of medium length ever written in Canada."[34] This praise derives not only from its technical virtuosity: the flexible pentameter line with a varying number of syllables, the skillful use of alliteration, "the long striding stanzas"[35] that suggest both the physical characteristics of its hero and of the mountains themselves, but from the inherent interest of the story itself. The old theme of an athlete dying young is here set in a poem that evokes better than any other the splendor and danger of the Rockies so that music, scenic beauty, and classic tragedy combine in one polished and harmonious entity. E. J. Pratt was the first critic to point out how Birney alternated between broad canvas observations and a close-up attention to detail,[36] an observation that applies to the story line as much as it does to the natural imagery; the day-by-day details of the boys' lives in the mountains — the flavor of wild raspberries, the shape of a trilobite, the sound of a rodent piping among the rocks — are counterpointed by the ever-present challenge of the Finger, the omnipresent threat of death, the necessity for making moral choices. As Birney himself has said, "['David'] is basically an imagined story shaped around the theme of the duality of human experience as symbolized ... by mountain-climbing — the hair's breadth between, on the one hand, beauty and the exhilaration of being alive, and on the other fear and nightmare and death and the static dumb hostility of the non-human world. More specifically, it's about the role of tragedy in the maturation of youth."[37]

Part of "David"'s dramatic impact derives from its conversational tone; the most dramatic and tragic events are recounted in a calm, reflective voice that leads the reader to identify with the narrator and hence to accept his point of view. This is a technique that Birney uses widely in his narrative poems; the conversational tone lends a note of characteristic understatement to the exploits of Conrad Kain, underscores the dignity of the speech of the Salish chief, and throws into dramatic relief the anguished tale of the Australian professor in "the gray woods exploding." Moreover, the conversational tone lends a note of authority or omniscience to the narrator's voice: because he is unmoved by the events that he recounts he appears to be superior to those events; what has happened has been a logical, if sometimes tragic, unfolding of the universe. Thus, Birney's narrative poems combine the antiquarian's interest in detail with a dispassionate and almost olympian view of life and death. The vivid evocations of the minutiae of life in a Salish village or in the Australian outback or in the high Rockies are used to underscore a world-view that is tragic and uncertain even when it is most enticing.

VIII   *The Craft So Long to Learn*

Birney's development as a poet has been remarkable considering that he only began writing appreciable amounts of poetry when he was in his late thirties. An even more remarkable fact is that although some of his most enduring work was published in *David and Other Poems* he has gone on to perfect himself in new techniques and to produce poetry of great power and variety. As Milton Wilson once said, "Birney is the exception to the Canadian rule that poets don't mature (they just repeat themselves or give up)."[38] In Birney's case the stilted diction of "On Going to the Wars" has given place to the lyricism of "on her twenty-sixth birthday," punctuation and capitalization have been replaced by the breathing space and the unobtrusive lower case, the poem as picture has overtaken the formal lyrics of his early years, and the language has become pungent, colloquial, free-wheeling. As Pacey says, Birney's style is "...not brilliant but persuasive, drawing sustenance from the idioms of Canadian speech.... Casual, unspectacular, but never slipshod, it has a loose, loping power that covers a lot of ground in a remarkably short time."[39] All of this speaks of a poet who has been in a constant state of change and development for four decades, adapting his style to the events and technology of the outside world and refining his poetic technique in the light of new experience without becoming addicted for very long to any fad.

Birney began his poetic career in reaction to "the curse of pedantry and obscurantism which [had] beset all verse" in the previous two decades; he was especially offended by the "obscurity that became a cult with Eliot's 'Waste Land,' [was] elaborated into a fashion by the Auden group and [which was] now observed as a duty by their disciples at home and abroad."[40] Although his own early work occasionally suffered from "a tendency to lapse into bookishness or priggishness,"[41] as in the case of "On Going to the Wars" and "Eagle Island," generally speaking Birney has adhered to the concept of the poet as a man speaking to men. His poetry is written to be read, preferably aloud, to audiences composed of all sorts and conditions of people, and this is what Birney has striven to do, especially in the last two decades; he has made a career of reading his poetry in every conceivable location. His desire to communicate by means of the spoken word has obliged him to adhere to the principles of clarity and of simplicity of expression and to adopt a conversational tone even when he is expressing the most controversial ideas.

Birney's experience as a journalist, combined with his love of roaming about, permitted him to convert his experiences into poems; the "observer's stance" was a natural complement to the curiosity and restlessness that led him to resume his travels in the early 1950s, and out of that combination came his poems on Mexico, the Caribbean, and South America. Although his poems almost invariably are a commentary upon some aspect of the human condition — a purely descriptive poem like "State of Sonora" is a rarity — the scenic details are always sharp and accurate. The reader experiences the dusty poverty of the Cuzco barrios, the lushness of the Jamaican rain forest, the loneliness of the tavern on the Hellespont.

As a result of Birney's insistence upon experiencing life to the full, his eagerness to stay in contact with the young, and his persistent polishing of his craft it has been accurately said that "the poetry is like the man — youthful without being young, mature without being mellow, formal and fluid at the same time...."[42] Birney's craft in fact has become representative of everything he has striven for and cherished in his life, and at the end instead of becoming a querulous old man he has gone leaping joyfully among the young poets, searching and questioning and trying out the newest techniques of poetry to express his horror and his delight at the world around him.

CHAPTER 7

Conclusion: People and Politics

I   *The Lonely Observer*

IN the 1940s Birney and some of his contemporaries — F. R. Scott, A. M. Klein, and P. K. Page — had begun to define a new attitude in Canadian poetry; where Canadian poets in the nineteenth century had tended to settle for a glorification of nature's beauties and the morally invigorating challenge of the frontier, Birney and the others "...sought in man's own mental and social world for a subject matter they can no longer find in the beauty of nature — a beauty that seems either deceptive or irrelevant."[1] Thus, poems like "David" and "Climbers" acknowledge the beauty of the landscape while they underline its harshness and indifference to the existence of man. Similarly, Birney carefully describes the jeweled landscape of a Nova Scotia winter in "ARRIVALS — Wolfville" —

> a snowscape
> clean and cosy as any Christmas card
> the small firs like spunwhite candy
> spaced on the ice-cream hillocks

— but this observation of the natural scene is only a backdrop upon which Birney projects the experience of a man's death. More to the point, "ARRIVALS — Wolfville" expresses most succinctly Birney's awareness of the solitude of the human condition. The train passengers who alight to see the body of the man whom their train has killed are

> ... anonymous one to the other
> but our breaths write on the air
> the kinship of being alive
> surrounding the perfect stranger....

142

It is not only the dead who are perfect strangers to one another. The title of "four feet between" is an ironic reference to the fact that Birney and the big old Fijian stand only four feet apart as they struggle to communicate while in fact their thought patterns and their backgrounds leave them light ages away from each other. The title also refers to the fact that between them they have four feet, but even this is a barrier to their understanding of each other; the "civilized" man's feet are cut to shreds by the coral while the "primitive" man is unharmed: "...most of all he couldnt understand what hurt my feet." Finally, by making the Fijian laugh at a witticism, Birney manages to achieve some kind of a rapport, but it is a small dividend considering the effort he has had to make.

This consciousness of man's confusion in the presence of his fellows also provides the theme for "A Walk in Kyoto." In this poem sex is a metaphor for truth or reality, but it is Birney's problem to decipher the complex riddle of a strangely inverted world. He does not know whether the magnolia in his room is male or female; the resident Deity is hermaphroditic; the actors in the *kabuki* and *takarazuka* plays are male and female transvestites; the "small bowed body" of the country itself seems to be symbolized by Birney's innmaid, or is it in fact vigorous and masculine? If Birney can penetrate the disguises surrounding flower, deity, actors, country, he will be free to communicate with the people and not have to "stand hunched / and clueless like a castaway in the shoals of [his] room." Then, as in "Cartagena de Indias," Birney is abruptly provided with a flash of insight. The maid silently points over his shoulder to where a small boy is flying a kite in the shape of a golden carp, a traditional Japanese symbol of virility.[2] Suddenly the riddle of this mysterious nation is resolved and an answer provided for the question of

> Where in these alleys jammed with competing waves
> of signs in two tongues and three scripts
> can the simple song of a man be heard?

The boy's act, specifically masculine and clearly sexual —

> a carp is rising   golden and fighting
> thrusting its paper body up from the fist
> of a small boy

— is one which unites him with boys and men everywhere. His kite, rising "higher / and higher   into the endless winds of the world" is a symbol of man's ability to pass over the oceans of ignorance and carry messages to his fellow man.

Still, for every small triumph of this sort there are any number of instances in which Birney is forced to recognize the difficulty if not the impossibility of establishing communications. Too often the barriers of language or custom or economic privilege stand between one man and another. Sometimes, as in "Turbonave Magnolia," a stupid racist regulation may be blamed for interrupting a blossoming friendship; sometimes, as in "the gray woods exploding," Birney's instinctive gesture of sympathy is rebuffed out of human pride and fear of getting hurt; more often Birney simply admits that loneliness is the natural condition of man.

This recognition, coupled with Birney's characteristic sense of ironic detachment, tends to set him in the observer's stance, watching, assessing, yet willing to accept friendship if it comes or express love if he feels it. "campus theatre steps," for example, is a pastiche of excerpts from theater posters and the noises of the world moving freely about its business on foot, in cars, and on trains, set over against the sight of a woman in a wheelchair being laboriously hauled up the steps of the theater. The poet silently observes the suffering of the individual in the presence of an indifferent world bent upon seeking its own pleasure and takes a couple of the blaring poster headlines to express his apocalyptic vision of what will become of such a society: "Tomorrow at 8:30 : : : the Griffins are / COMING."

It is logical therefore that one should look through Birney's eyes, as it were, to deduce who it is that he admires in the human race. Surprisingly, considering his avowedly pessimistic view of humanity, there is a considerable number of such people, and they include everyone from small children to aborigines, from simple working men to explorers, and certainly one of the most striking of these groups is the series of young men — David, Mickey in the short story "Mickey Was a Swell Guy," Conrad Kain, Gordon Saunders, Joe Harris — who crop up regularly in Birney's works. Despite their youth they tend to be mature, patient, kindly, generous, and physically robust. Like Beowulf, Percival, and other heroes of antiquity they learn about life through intense personal suffering. In fact, only those people who suffer, including the young professor in "the gray woods exploding," actually learn about life; the rest tend to be immature or to remain vapid tourists gaping uncomprehendingly upon a life that streams past them.

Occasionally one of these young men makes the journey into self-knowledge alone. Gordon Saunders does this both physically and spiritually in *Down the Long Table;* the long trip by freight train from Toronto to Vancouver teaches the aloof young academic something about his own country and its inhabitants, but it also initiates him into the world of political and economic reality.

Joe Harris and the professor of "the gray woods exploding" also make their journeys alone in the sense that death has left them bereft of their loved ones, but both are all the more poignant figures in that they are apparently condemned to continue their journeys forever. The young professor is living "a long way off / So he's still alive in a way somewhere," and the disembodied voice of Joe Harris still pleads, "Which are my sins, padre?"

More often, Birney's young men are accompanied by an even younger follower who also matures and loses something of his innocence as a result of what happens to the principal character. Thus, David is accompanied by Bob, Mickey by the unnamed narrator of the story, Kain by a series of fellow mountain-climbers who are at least junior to him in terms of experience, and Turvey trots doggedly in the track of his hero, Mac, learning, under the veil of humorous predicaments, progressively more bitter lessons. And the bitterest lesson of all for these disciples is the fact of their hero's mortality, and their own, for whether Birney's young men make their journey alone or in the company of a disciple, in the end they are destroyed. Gordon Saunders is brought down by old political enemies; Joe Harris, Mickey, and Mac are killed in one war or another; David chooses his own death rather than life as an invalid; the young professor is hounded by a relentless bureaucracy and the memory of his beloved wife.

In many of these cases, Birney employs the destruction of the young man to make a specifically political statement: the lives of Conrad Kain, Mickey, and Joe Harris are blighted by a perverted economic system which denies them food and education in their youth and any hope of social advancement in later life. They are all, in one way or another, pawns in a system that crushes their potential to live fully as human beings. Yet, the lives and deaths of Birney's young heroes are sometimes dignified by a grandeur of surprisingly godlike and even Christlike quality. Mickey battles for the weak and helpless schoolboys and is wounded in such an

encounter; Kain is the good shepherd of the mountains who injured
no man:

> He seized his land for no sovereign
> and left it uncivilized still.
> He was reckless only in rescuing others
> and his proudest record was this:
> that on stormiest edge
> or through deepest crevasse
> he led no man to his hurt.

But much more striking is the Christian symbolism in "David" and
"Joe Harris." David accepts the blame for Bob's mistake; both
David and Joe Harris are wounded in the side; the counterpoint to
Joe's words is provided by a chaplain intoning the Christian service
for the burial of the dead.

Still, if one reads these two last poems more closely, one realizes
that the references to Christianity are misleading. David's death is
more suited to a Stoic than a Christian, and Joe denies the existence
of a God who can restore him to life: "Nor is there any Lord that
will close the wound in my own side." Perhaps the key to these two
poems lies in a third: "Takkakaw Falls." The river, clearly linked
to the ancient river gods, like David loses its foothold in the mountains and plunges to its death, whence after a time it is reborn to
rise and thunder once again. The underlying implication of the
poems about Birney's young men dying young is that they have
become transmuted by their deaths; they have left an ineradicable
mark upon the people they have known and have become gods in a
New World Parnassus reserved for heroes.

These young men are also linked by their attributes to the explorers whom Birney so clearly admires and who keep cropping up in
his poetry. Perhaps his own insatiable wanderlust made him feel a
kinship with these men, whether they are figments of his imagination like David and Gordon Saunders or real-life explorers like
Cook, Bering, and Bingham. What they all have in common is a
restless desire to search and discover even at the risk of their own
lives. Birney's early "Atlantic Door" invokes the memories of
"Gilbert's hearties and Jellicoe's," and its companion-piece,
"Pacific Door," acknowledges the sometimes inadvertent heroism
that helped to open the West Coast and the Pacific:

long pain and sweating courage chalked
such names as glimmer yet
Drake's crewmen scribbled here their paradise
and dying Bering lost in fog
turned north to mark us off from Asia still
Here cool Cook traced in blood his final bay.

This is the other side of the Birney who despairs of mankind because of its intransigence in the face of self-made disaster. Here he admires the human stubbornness, perseverance, curiosity, and intellectual power that lead men like Hiram Bingham to rediscover lost treasures like Machu Picchu.

Birney also seems to feel this sense of sympathetic rapport with those simple farmers or workers whose labor lends them an ennobling quality. Sometimes, as in "Joe Harris," the ethos of the working man is direct and poignant: "It is a brief sleep only I need.... And after that to work as never before, in my own land, with my own hand and brain, and to eat the fruits I have grown." Or, in the thoughts of the "Man on a Tractor" who, unlike Joe Harris, has survived the war and returned to work his own land: "I have come through with my hands and feet / and won the right to plow black earth of my own." Sometimes Birney's consciousness of something decent in simple men is focused by the fact of death. In "ARRIVALS — Wolfville" his habitual sarcasm is muted as he acknowledges the fragility of human beings in the face of natural forces. Even the dialect-speaking locals, usually the object of Birney's satire and contempt, here have something decent and humane about them; one of them gathers up the scattered papers of the dead lawyer, another brings a blanket from the train to cover the shattered body. Sometimes, as in "the gray woods exploding," Birney uses his own experiences as a laboring man to bridge an otherwise insurmountable gap between himself and another man. The young professor remains shy and aloof until Birney reaches out to him with stories of his own youthful labors.

Yet, there is another dimension to Birney's sympathy for the worker: not every job requires the skill of a carpenter or a mountaineer. Some jobs — most, perhaps — never provide the satisfaction of conquering Mount Robson or fitting together a beautifully crafted cabinet or cross. The title of "The ebb begins from dream," for example, refers to the fact that the working masses form a huge tide that daily sweeps from the depths of sleep down to their workplaces and then ebbs wearily back to dreamland each evening. The tide imagery also suggests the manner in which the laboring life wears the individual down; from the flood tide of youth the incessant demands of toil reduce man to a neap tide, glad to trickle back to his final sleeping place and forgetful of the ideas and ideals which inspired him at his setting out. Despite the fact that the closing lines of the poem imply that there is a great, if unconscious, dream of a better and more fulfilling life present in all of mankind, too often the "morning vow" is forgotten in the weariness of the evening; the working man's promise to himself of a better world becomes

> salt evening weeds that lie
> and rot between the cracks of life
> and hopes that waterlogged will never link
> with land   but will be borne until they sink.

This awareness of the harsh and dehumanizing quality of modern industrial life is one of the factors that causes Birney to romanticize people and places from long ago and far away. "November Walk near False Creek Mouth" implies that the mead-tipplers of King Alfred's time and the "tiffin-takers" of British India were in some way aesthetically or even physically superior to Birney's Vancouver contemporaries who drink their "fouroclock chainstore tea." Something of this tendency can be detected in Birney's poems about exotic places — Peru, the Caribbean, the South Pacific — all of which contain echoes of a belief in the grandeur of the "natural man." Margaret Atwood noticed that Al Purdy in *North of Summer* and Farley Mowat in *The People of the Deer* identify with those Indians or Eskimos whose tribal life has been destroyed by the white man's "civilization," i.e., those aborigines who are dead and who exist only in artifacts and legend, not the degenerate, contemporary, living ones.[3] The same thing can be said of Birney's poems, including *Trial of a City,* "the mammoth corridors," "what's so big about GREEN?" and "The shapers: Vancouver"; he does not have a living Indian anywhere in his work. What is more, in "charité esperance et foi" Birney's ironic admiration of the savagery of the three Indian girls and of their conduct in the face of Samuel de Champlain's efforts to civilize them is exactly the opposite of Pratt's attitude toward the Indians in "Brebeuf and His Brethren." In Birney's estimation the white man deserved all the suffering he got from the natives.

Yet, if his work is taken as a whole, no one could accuse Birney of being rabidly anti-Canadian or of seeing all foreigners or aborigines in a totally flattering light. Although he never becomes rapturous about Canadians, and though many of his poems like "Sixsided square: Actopan" and "To a Hamilton (Ont.) lady thinking to travel" are marred by a condescending irony in favor of the natives, he does come to recognize that other people have their defects too. The speaker in "Sinaloa" is clearly in favor of industrial exploitation of his own country; the Japanese in "Small port in the outer Fijis" are as rapacious as any "northamericans"; while Birney and the old Fijian in "Four feet between" do not condescend to each other or even overrate each other. Birney's early works certainly reveal a typically Canadian naiveté in his tendency to overestimate the moral qualities of Jamaicans, Mexicans, and French Canadians, but with the passage of the years this has been replaced by a more balanced judgment, a willingness to take his friends wherever he can find them. Where once his poems of friendship were directed to people in Belgium, Holland, or the Caribbean, he now writes love poems to a girl in Toronto and friendly banter to a fellow poet in Ameliasburg, Ontario. Foreigners may still be his friends, but the fact of being a foreigner is no longer a necessary condition for earning Birney's admiration.

A similar modification has been extended to Birney's view of the rich and rapacious. When *Now Is Time* was published, E. K. Brown remarked in a review of the book that for Birney the life of the rich ". . . is seen from below angrily, and without any real sense of [their] motive. The dramatic quality of Mr. Birney's poetry suffers by the contrast between his ever-ready sympathy with the poor, a sympathy grounded in understanding, and his summary unconvincing presentation of their masters. His bitterness of mood forces its way into almost everything he writes, sometimes to give it great energy and vigour, but often to weaken a note of delight or triumph, or to destroy a touch of reality."[4] In the context of poems like "Hands," "Joe Harris," and "Man on a Tractor" these remarks were certainly valid, although the same volume contained poems such as "Anglosaxon Street" and "And the Earth Grow Young Again," poems which either were not directed against the rich or which specifically satirized the follies of the working class. In any case, in the twenty years between the publication of *Now Is Time* and *Selected Poems* Birney's emphasis upon the larceny of the upper classes gradually was transmuted into a stance which committed him to the defense of no party, group, or class, but which rather permitted him to underline the moral failures common to mankind as a whole. As a reviewer of the later book said, "He points constantly and consistently to the contradiction of what would seem to be the legitimate human interests of happiness and fulfillment by the vulgarity, vacuity, sterility — and what would appear to be the wilful plain foolishness — of contemporary purposes and aspirations."[5] Two years earlier, Birney had explained his own sense of identification with Ginsberg, Ferlinghetti, Corso, and the other Beat poets by saying that "it was a means of passionate identification, by all of us, poets and non-poets, with resentment — an all-out expression of hate, hate of ourselves and detestation of the whole lousy fear-ridden world our ancestors have made, and of our own pious smug daily defence of it."[6] In his 1948 poem "Images in place of logging" Birney had compared human beings and their machines to destructive animals and insects; in "Cucarachas in paradise" (1969) he suggested that cockroaches compare favorably with human beings. Taken in its entirety, then, Birney's poetry does not really show a consistent class bias; it tends to reveal anger and disappointment with the shortcomings of the human race as a whole.

Certainly one of the shortcomings that angers him the most is man's habit of pillaging the environment and exploiting his fellows. Even his earliest poems, like "The Road to Nijmegen," are passionate condemnations not just of the ravages of war but of the misuse of man's intellectual powers. Anyone who has seen the shattered landscape and the starving children of one war should, theoretically, be capable of preventing another such tragedy, but even then Birney was admitting that mankind was on a "road / that arrives at no future" and that he himself was tortured by the "guilt / in the griefs of the old / and the graves of the young." Then, after he had returned home and seen New Brunswick, a "great green girl grown sick / with man," had read the "page of Gaspé" like an old illuminated manuscript carelessly scribbled upon by modern man's factories and banks, and had observed the desolate "Images in place of logging," he came to something of a watershed in his expressions of contempt for the ravages created by man exploiting nature. "Way to the West" (1965) continues in a more fierce and explicit form Birney's condemnation of a rapacious mankind. Up to this point he had permitted himself the luxury of ironic laughter at foolish developers like the speaker in "Sinaloa." After all, there is a good deal to be said for the man's point of view; the people of Sinaloa are poor, and a breakwater would be economically better than palm trees; sugarcane plantations are more important than egrets; a grain elevator or a boxcar full of rice is much better than an old fort when one is hungry. The speaker is perfectly correct, from a developer's standpoint, in preferring tractors, refrigerator trucks, and new highways to machetes, oxcarts, and "bugumbilla." The only point that he is missing is the one made by Birney in "Prosperity in Poza Rica," namely that wealth derived from the uncontrolled exploitation of natural resources all too seldom trickles down to the poor and hungry. In this poem, oil brings quick profits to lawyers, drillers, and casual laborers, but a few miles away the Indian farmer still scrabbles for his living, plowing his land with a sharpened stick.

By the time he wrote "Way to the West," however, the softening element of humor had disappeared. Sudbury is evoked as a perfect example of man's ability to create hell on earth. The images are all selected for their shock effect: young demons drag-race their shrieking cars through the sulfurous atmosphere; older ones spit gobs of brown slime on the pavement; with smarting eyes Birney notices that the local rock formations look like "glazed guts on a butcher's marble." Outside of town, with still twenty miles of this horror to endure, the travelers stop. There is no sound because all nature is dead. They are shocked to realize that in the background the murmuring of a river can be heard; until now its sound had been obscured by the roaring of the pandemonium through which they have just passed. Birney has painted other portraits of this same area, notably in "North of Superior," which dwells upon its emptiness and solitude, but at least in "North of Superior" the land still has a certain integrity, however barren, of its own. There may not be any knights or dragons in these sparse reaches of rock and spindly trees, but the seasons come and go; the odd trapper follows the track of other living creatures; trees, flowers, and even lichens do live out a natural cycle. In "Way to the West," on the other hand, man has ensured the destruction of even this simple life cycle, and implicitly has condemned himself as well. Aside from the beer-sodden residents coughing their lungs out, the slogans about "Centre of Free Enterprise" are linked to images of the battlefield, Cape Kennedy, and Vietnam. Free enterprise in the form of unbridled greed seems to involve death and damnation on an international scale.

In contrast to the traditional enthusiasm of poets like Carl Sandburg for the spectacle of North American industrial development, Birney is more impressed by the fact of man's becoming a victim of that which he had wrought to serve him. The last line of "Oil Refinery," "Eala! we are lost   in the spell of his loopings," is the petroleum-based society's cry of despair when it realizes how it has entangled itself; there is no victory or even heroic death for industrial man.

Birney also came to admit that the exploiters and despoilers of nature are not just "northamericans"; they come in all shapes and colors. From the eager Mexican babbling on about "developing" the state of Sinaloa to the Australian businessmen busily stripping coral off the Great Barrier Reef in "the gray woods exploding" to the Japanese fishing conglomerates sweeping the Pacific Ocean clear of tuna, swordfish, and even sharks, Birney expresses his disgust at the despoliation of a planet. The poem "a small port in the outer Fijis" is especially pertinent here since a variety of races, all of them supposedly civilized, have combined to rape a paradise. The Japanese fishing company is working in close partnership with the Australian port authorities and the New Zealand fishmeal processors. Meanwhile,

> The British are all back in Suva
> plotting to set Fiji free
> The Indians are keeping the shops   & procreating
>
> There are no Fijians in view.

Although Birney's view of humanity is a despairing one, it is often softened or modified when he deals with a specific human being: David, Conrad Kain, Joe Harris. Like Swift, he loves Peter and Paul but detests mankind as a verminous entity. In a sense, the Swiftian analogy can be extended: Birney's vitriolic poems are his *Drapier's Letters,* an attempt to save mankind's moral coinage from becoming totally debased. In "the mammoth corridors" he reflects upon the fact that "from my own lusts and neckties and novels / from ulcers   vitamins   bulletins *accidia* / i lie unshielded." *Accidia* is the ultimate form of moral debasement, a state of spiritual sloth and indifference and one to which Birney is well aware that modern man is all too prone.

Birney once said that E. J. Pratt's poetry had been shaped by the belief "that we are men, uniquely nonanimal, and capable of great devotion and splendour either in the preservation or in the destruction of ourselves as men."[7] The other major poet whom Birney seems to admire most strongly is Chaucer, another cheerful humanist, and yet Birney himself, except in rare instances like "Vancouver Lights," seems incapable of sharing these poets' good-natured acceptance of human folly and their admiration of human grandeur. His work tends rather to be marked by the bitter experience of the Depression, the intellectual constipation of academe, and the facts of war, nuclear proliferation, and ecological disaster. As a result his final judgment of the human race is harsh, often bitter, and sometimes despairing.

II *Politics: "A Creed, Not a Dogma"*

From his earliest years Birney had been exposed to those factors which contributed to the radical political views he was to adopt in adulthood. The sturdy nonconforming spirit of his mother's people, his father's beliefs resulting from a lifetime as a Canadian working man, Birney's own exposure to political corruption as a student in Vancouver, and the political activism of the Depression years all contributed to his adoption of the Marxist outlook as a young man.[8] When World War II broke out, Birney felt that if the conflict were to have any sense or justification at all it would have to be in the political realm.

The possibility that men might find the strength and unity to reform a society which had produced such debacles as the Great Depression lent a tinge of hope to the prospect of war, and it is this hope which colors those few optimistic passages in Birney's poetry of the 1940s. In "On Going to the Wars" he was able to write confidently that

> No hell unspilled by lords of war
> Upon the people's flesh has ever
> Parched the human heart's endeavour,
> The human will to love and truth.

Both "Joe Harris" and "For Steve" are preoccupied with revising the social order. In "Joe Harris" the thoughts of a soldier killed at Dieppe are interpolated with passages from *The Shortened Service for the Burial of the Dead as Approved for Use in the Canadian Army.* The soldier recalls the events of a life which lasted only twenty-nine years and which included suffering, deprivation, roaming about in a near-hopeless search for work and for some meaning in life, a brief moment of married love, and then the trip overseas to his death. Unlike the soldier in Rupert Brooke's "If I should die," with his fatalistic and even willing acceptance of death for a beloved country and social order, Joe Harris beseeches "that the world we have builded, and that has brought us to this, will perish with me." Joe is willing to accept peacefully his own destruction "only if such as my son may go in no fear of mousy hunger, of yard-cops, and the slammed door in a Canada mildewed with the fat and unheeding." What Joe Harris desires is a socialist society based upon love, reason, and generosity: "Yet it was nothing I learned in pews or glossy books that brought me here or availed me in these times, but only the gods that live in such words as freedom, and truth, love and reason. . . . I am dead for a creed, not a dogma." To some extent at least the poem implies Birney's belief that such a society would emerge from the ashes of the war.

In any case, it would be a mistake to exaggerate the extent of Birney's optimism even during the early stages of the war. His very first book of poems contained, among others, such pessimsitic works as "Hands," "Monody for a Century," and "Dusk on English Bay," all of which to a greater or lesser degree are forecasts of the impending slaughter. The title of "Monody for a Century," for example, suggests that World War II will be the last significant act of the twentieth century. "Hands" is a bitter series of contrasts between the relative innocence of the natural world and the depraved purposes of the human intellect. "Dusk on English Bay" gloomily concedes that there is no Joshua capable of arresting the destructive forces that man has unleashed in the world. In other words, Birney's occasional expressions of hope for a better social order after the war are counterbalanced by the unhappy realization that there may be no world left after this particular war; in such a situation there is very little point in arguing over differing political theories or planning for a better world. Birney's essential pessimism about the future of society is summed up in "War Winters." The miseries caused by the wretched winter of 1942 are not so much a result of the natural laws ruling the solar system as they are of man's folly; the "winter" to which the poem refers is in the heart of man as much as it is part of the natural world.

Whatever faint optimism Birney felt about the possibility of reforming the social order can also be detected in the companion poems "Man is a Snow" and "...Or a Wind," which he wrote in the two years immediately following the war. The "snow" of the first poem refers to the coldness of man's heart: "Man is a snow that winters / his own heart's cabin," and the "useless windows" are his eyes, through which he refuses to see the "lost world" of beauty, myth, and social justice. The second poem, however, suggests that a different course of action is open to mankind if it refuses to be governed by selfishness and acts instead with fraternity and courage. "...Or a Wind" tells us that knowledge can be gained through suffering; mankind's "acid tears" can eat away "these mountain walls," the walls of ignorance, prejudice, and oppression that have kept man in misery for ages. As long as there is life, "something renews us" and in the end "we may yet roar free.../ the great wind of humanity flowing free.../ streaming over the future." This seems to be substantial evidence that as late as 1947 Birney still held out some hope for a new political and social order.

Still, it would be a mistake to overrate this small degree of optimism. Birney was perfectly aware of what could happen to Western society, and in poems like "Ulysses" and "Status Quo" he outlines some of the dangers awaiting an unreformed world. The "soldier" and "sailor" of "Ulysses" are the Canadian veterans, men like the farmer in "Man on a Tractor." Birney warns them not to be seduced too easily by "Peace, the bitchy Queen." The "old dog Time" has granted them one last chance to establish a better rule; failing that, the "phony lords and "suitors" — the prewar Establishment — will be only too quick to enslave the country and its workers once again. On a more universal scale, Birney warns the world at large of what is sure to happen unless profiteering, hate-mongering, racism, narrow nationalism, and the unequal distribution of wealth are brought under control.

Birney had actually not been affiliated with any political dogma since he broke with the Trotskyite movement in 1941, and in a sense the poems included in *Now Is Time* and *Strait of Anian* were nearly his last hurrah as an optimist for the human race. After this, he rarely expressed a belief in the powers of the human reason. By a curious irony it was not so much the events of World War II as it was his continued observation and experience of the human race that exhausted whatever limited store of optimism he had started out with.

The critics later commented on "Birney's war poetry of the forties with its sense of involvement from the western edge of things, its Canadian scapegoats for a war they never made and yet were somehow responsible for: ...its equivocal relations between (and even identity of) guilt and innocence."[9] This awareness of the working man as a pawn of the militarist system is reflected in much of Birney's work written in the late 1940s, as, for example, in the very fine poem "Moon Down Elphinstone," about two young men who hide out in the mountains in order to escape military service. One of them sneaks back into town to see his friend's sister, finds that she has jilted him, gets drunk, and is picked up by the military police and forced into the army. Some time later he goes back up Mount Elphinstone to tell his friend that his mother is dying; the friend sees only a soldier coming for him and shoots him. When he realizes who the soldier is, he kills himself and the two young men lie together, unburied, in the rain.

This remarkable poem sums up all the sense of fear, frustration, and impotence experienced by ordinary working men in the face of a political system so vast and implacable as to assume the dimensions of Fate. The poem is technically a ballad, but instead of having the aristocratic heroes of the traditional ballad its heroes are New World proletarians; like Turvey, they are poor working stiffs rather than Young Lochinvar or Bonnie Dundee. The action, set in the coastal mountains, ends with typically North American violence, and thematically the poem deals with the perturbing questions of civil disobedience and Canada's fighting of foreign wars in the service of an imperial power. Whether these men serve that power or whether they try to avoid it, it kills them in the end. In "Man on a Tractor," "Joe Harris," and "For Steve" there was in every case a living survivor to carry on the struggle, to set right the system that had destroyed the dead soldier. In "Moon Down Elphinstone" there are no survivors; the poem ends in death, rain, and silence.

Most of Birney's work from 1949 to 1960 is marked by his horror at the nuclear calamity hanging over the head of mankind, contrasted by his enunciation of an existential belief in the power of the human heart to find a way through political and social chaos. If, for example, there is a form of socialism implicit in Conrad Kain's actions — he leaves home to help his family and to escape a stratified society, and his personal qualities help him cross the barriers of wealth and privilege in the New World — it is incidental to the central motif of a man succeeding as part of the human race because of his selflessness and his indomitable courage.

These same qualities are fundamental to the character of Mrs. Anyone, the heroine of *Trial of a City*. Mrs. Anyone does not subscribe to any political creed; in fact, it is her totally nonpolitical stance that saves the day for humanity. Mr. Legion, who questions the successive witnesses in an effort to shape a defense for the capitalist free-market system, only manages to elicit the most damning evidence regarding the effects of such a system. Mr. Powers, the prosecutor, on the other hand, represents a form of suicidal, world-weary nihilism; he is that part of the human spirit which bases itself upon pure reason and, being rationally convinced that man can never produce anything good, resigns itself to self-destruction. Both Legion and Powers base their arguments upon reason and logic, but the deadly impasse which their logic creates can only be resolved by a suprarational, i.e., an existentialist, position based solely upon the sanctity of life and the power of love.

It has been suggested that Legion is a fraud because he is in reality not a member of the working masses but a "folksy capitalist" who exploits them. His expulsion by Mrs. Anyone at the end of the play and her preempting of the name of Legion may thus be seen as representing Birney's long-standing dream of the overthrow of the capitalist exploiters by the masses.[10] It is more likely that *Trial of a City* is one of the works which marks the era in which Birney quit propagandizing for socialism or any other "ism," realizing, like Mrs. Anyone, that the world wags on regardless of philosophic or political systems, that life is more important than any system. He would continue to remark, often bitterly, upon the ironies and injustices of contemporary life but he no longer advocated any formal party line.

Something of this attitude is also reflected in the outlook of Gordon Saunders in *Down the Long Table*. Having awakened to the truth about political parties and dogmas, Gordon Saunders still must face the dilemma of what he as an individual can do for the welfare of humanity; does he feel that action of some sort is necessary or even justified? The questions are made all the more urgent by the fact that the time is now the early 1950s and he is facing an inquiry into his activities of twenty years earlier. Like Mrs. Anyone he has a great deal at stake. She was faced with an omnipotent force threatening the life of the race; Saunders, now an eminently successful man, faces professional destruction and possibly jail. Like Mrs. Anyone he responds, not rationally, but existentially:

I believe in man . . ., even in [his persecutors], for somewhere in them, as in me, is the power, however denied, to achieve the grandeur of the thinking beast, to hope and to imagine, to adventure into change, to create beauty and to share it, and in self-denial itself to assert the importance of their separate selves and the inconsequence of their mortality.[11]

It was a fortunte thing that Birney could still believe in the power of the individual spirit, because during this decade there was much evidence of the failure of mankind to act in concert. He was very depressed by the prospect of nuclear war[12] and by the political situation in the world as a whole. In 1957 he concluded a survey of the North American theater, which he considered, with the exception of O'Neill's work, to consist of diverting pap, by saying that the floundering drama was a manifestation of the fact that the world lacked a positive creed:

We know only negatives — that our democratic way of life is not very good and not very democratic but it is not as bad or as undemocratic as the totalitarian way of life; that there is no creed which can yet unify the world and no science, exact or political, which without a creed, may not destroy us. We do not know even whether anything in human affairs is really either comic or tragic any more.[13]

Here, as in his fiction and poetry, he comforts himself with a belief in the existential power of the human spirit, for in another article he says that the world needs and can attain "that necessary leadership not by a Leader but, as it were, by masses of leaders, men and women who do not necessarily draw their strength from the too-rare commodity of saintliness, nor from the too-abundant reservoir of ruthlessness, but from rational faith based on world knowledge, and some desperate hope, and much charity for that world."[14]

This concept of the religion of man may be discerned in Birney's poem "El Greco: Espolio," first published in 1960. In a sense, the carpenter who is the focus of all eyes in the painting is guilty of the crucifixion; he is a member of the society that condones such a method of execution and he earns part of his living from the manufacture of crosses. Yet he, like Conrad Kain, is essentially apolitical; the fine points of the law are a matter of indifference to him. By his devotion to his craft, and by the skill with which he works, he transcends political and legal considerations. He and Christ are related through the fact that they are both carpenters, and on another level they are the kin of all humanity through their honesty and devotion to what they do. The soldiers, servants of the political hierarchy, may dice and squabble over the prisoner's garments but the honest workman is exonerated from guilt and freed from political entanglements by his preoccupation with doing well the task which has been set for him.

Essentially, the poem deals with the question of whether religion derives from man or from God; the gesture which Christ is making in the carpenter's direction is one of "curious beseechment"; Christ may be seeking "forgiveness or blessing." For Birney, the only religion that exists is that of the honest craftsman working as best he knows how according to a set of rules that derive from his own spirit.

Birney's experiences in Latin America form the basis of many of his political observations in the early 1960s, possibly because the effects of an inequitable system are much more obvious in that region than they are in the industrialized nations. In Latin America the evidences of poverty, illiteracy, and disease are apparent on every street corner while in North America and Europe they tend to be camouflaged or hidden away out of sight in ghettos. The vivid contrasts between rich and poor and the violent measures taken by the rich to maintain their status must have reminded Birney of the bad old days of the 1930s. In "Cartagena de Indias," for example, he makes the point that the poor and not-poor form two distinct constituencies, one of which seeks to interact with the other and one which seeks to avoid its social and economic responsibilities. As a result, human beings are reduced to the status of plunderers. Cartagena was long the target of pirates like Drake and Cole and later traded the independence it won under Bolívar to the power of the multinational corporations and the armed forces. Now, Birney, as a tourist, feels that he is one of a new generation of plunderers, profiting from the low tourist prices that result from the country's poverty, and being plundered in turn by the various hawkers and pitchmen who molest and shortchange him.

"Caracas" is another Latin American poem which deals with the theme of men being reduced to ciphers by the pressures of the capitalist system. Men, buildings, the national hero, all are reduced to numbers — "9-mile ooze of slums," "89 skyscrapers," "206 bones of Bolívar" — and the numbers ultimately become dollars or are equated to dollars, the "bright bloodsmell of / $$$$$" that draws the sharklike exploiters in their Cadillacs. The fact that the

country is the prey of exploiters reflects the persistent failure of
revolutions to assuage the woes of the masses. Bolívar's bright
promise, like that of the young priest in "Letter to a Cuzco Priest,"
has been swept aside as the monied interests ignore the declaration
of independence and the "7,000,000 lesser organisms" — their
countrymen — in the pursuit of profit.

The picturesque beauty of Latin America is therefore everywhere
overshadowed by the threat of revolutions past or to come. The
strawberries for which Irapuato is famous remind the poet of the
hearts torn out of living prisoners after the long succession of
battles fought there, tribe against tribe and nation against nation.
The "Sestina for the Ladies of Tehuantepec" sinuously uncovers
the menace for all mankind that is inherent in the human character;
the "gray iguana" of the poet's brain contains the elements of a
murdering dictator like Diaz; the radioactive hotsprings and the
earthquakes for which the area is noted are metaphors for the
nuclear explosives and the wars that the superpowers are capable of
unleashing upon each other. Here, as in "Letter to a Cuzco Priest,"
the dangers facing mankind must be staved off by man's own wit
and courage; no outside force can do it for him. In this case it is the
women of Tehunatepec who represent everything that is enduring,
beautiful, and hopeful in the human character.

Unfortunately, there is always the problem that people are too
intimidated by the regime, or else live too close to the ills of their
own society or are too ignorant to realize what is happening before
their very eyes. The speaker in "Most of a Dialogue in Cuzco" is
the typical tourist, willing to be hauled bodily over the Peruvian
mountains, to admire what the guide tells her to admire, and to
accept the opinions of the English-speaking guide, appointed by the
government, as to local conditions. It takes not only a poet, but
usually a foreign poet, to recognize the defects of a given society
and to have the opportunity to speak out against it. Cartagena's
Luis Lopez was in self-imposed exile for most of his life and thus
felt free to criticize, however benignly, the shortcomings of his
countrymen. In the case of Argentina the situation is much more
dangerous; a poet who criticizes too loudly is risking death or
imprisonment. Therefore, in "Buenos Aires: 1962" Birney is suggesting that only the Chilean poet Pablo Neruda has written with
satiric insight about the political oppression in the Argentine; the
Argentinian poets have all been effectively silenced.

If Birney was perturbed by what he saw in Latin America in the

1950s and 1960s, he was even more horrified by the war in Vietnam. "Looking from Oregon," which was written just after the American intervention in the Gulf of Tonkin, is a gloomy reflection upon the casual, thoughtless, recurrent fashion in which man wages war and invites his own disaster. The waves rolling in from the Pacific remind Birney of what is happening halfway around the world where they had their origin, and their recurrent motion is symbolic of the recurrence of warfare in human history. The poem is reminiscent of Matthew Arnold's "Dover Beach" in that the poet's musings include a fatalistic vision of an indifferent natural world, but at least the cruelties of that world involve no sense of guilt, whereas man's persistent movement toward the "thunderheads" of war and destruction necessarily produce an overwhelming sense of guilt and depression over the perversion of his powers of reason.

Birney's views on Canada's involvement in the Vietnam war are set forth in "i accuse us," a speech which he gave at an anti-Vietnam war rally in Toronto in 1967. To Birney, the Canadians are specialists "in waging / neither-war-nor-peace"; they are unique only in their "dynamic apathy." At the same time that they remain officially neutral on the Vietnamese war their industries are reaping huge profits selling war materiel to the United States. This hypocrisy vis-à-vis the foreign war is only a reflection of Canada's persistent hypocrisy regarding its domestic problems; while it pretends to be the peace-loving, unified inheritor of two cultural traditions, the British and the French, it is in fact a patchwork of hostile governments each disputing the authority of the national government. Its understanding of its cultural heritage is nebulous, and in the realm of foreign affairs it lacks even the United States' ruthless willingness to wage war openly.

Birney's progressive disenchantment with Canada and its internal squabbles is recorded in the various versions of "Canada: Case History" that he published between 1948 and 1972. The first version was a mildly satirical and fairly accurate musing upon the past and future problems of a vast young country. The prognosis was uncertain, but not hopeless. Twenty years later, Birney was moved to revise the poem for Canada's centennial year, and this time the satire was more scathing; there were references to failing health and moral turpitude. Then the violent aspect of the Quebec separatist movement inspired another version, and a fourth was published in 1972 in which Canada was now diagnosed as being "Schizoid for sure and now a sado-masochist." After this last bitter effort to express his disgust with Canada's international ineptitude and history of internal discord Birney finally withdrew permission for any of the four versions of the poem to be printed; he was "tired of being forced, by this jeremiad, to pose as a permanent sociological judge-and-jury of my own country...."[15]

The decade of the 1970s did nothing to reassure Birney about the political situation either on the national or the international level; if anything, he became even more vitriolic than before in his comments upon current events and the nature of man. In 1974 he told Al Purdy:

The U.S. is an imperial power, which is difficult to like. They are sloughing off whatever democracy they have left with succeeding waves of reaction, neo-fascism and imperialism. Nothing short of a major catastrophe will stop that drift. They may even be breaking up right now, while we are watching. We in Canada must have the courage and willingness to sacrifice and wait for the time when the U.S. will no longer be able to bully.[16]

This pessimism is reflected in his poetry: his perception of the natural beauty of the Firth of Forth is marred by the shadow of the American nuclear submarine lying beneath the bridge upon which he stands; the garrison mentality that has brought on all the misery and slaughter of the twentieth century is revealed in his "found paean to vancouver by rudyard kipling (1890)":

> ...what Vancouver wants
> is...
> a selection of big guns
> a couple of regiments of infantry,
> and later a big arsenal....

In the same volume, *what's so big about GREEN?,* there is a poem, "underkill," that brings into focus much of what has happened to the world since Birney published *David and Other Poems.* "underkill" is about an old trading tavern that used to draw tourists because it had been the scene of a spectacular murder. Now it is boarded up; it can no longer compete for public interest with the massive slaughter of the wars of the twentieth century and the ultimate prospect of total nuclear annihilation. People who used to be titillated at one man's murder now look for bigger things.

In an essay on several Canadian poets, Northrop Frye asks how one can define the Canadian character and answers the question by saying, in part,

We should expect in Canada ... a strong suspicion, not of the United States itself, but of the mercantilist Whiggery that won the Revolution and proceeded to squander the resources of a continent, being now engaged in squandering ours.... The Canadian point of view is at once more conservative and more radical than Whiggery, closer both to aristocracy and to democracy than to oligarchy.[17]

All this is very true of Birney; he has a fierce contempt, expressed both in poetry and prose, for northamerican "mercantile whiggery." *The Damnation of Vancouver* is based upon this theme, and if one considers that Vancouver is the most American of all Canadian cities, the point becomes even more important.

But what of Birney's democracy, and what of his aristocracy? His democracy has always been of the socialist type; as long as he held any hope whatever for a better political order, he insisted upon the development of a socialist democracy free of the cycles of poverty and warfare that had plagued the Western world throughout most of his lifetime. As for his aristocrats, they tend to be either dead or else they are natural objects: the mountains, the forests of coastal ranges, the changeless sea. These are phenomena which man at his best may admire and even worship; at his worst he may pollute and destroy them. The fact that Birney's human aristocrats, including the Salish chief in *Trial of a City,* the pre-Conquest Incas, and explorers like Cook and Bering, are all dead suggests that modern man is, after all, a fallen creature.

Notes and References

Chapter One

1. Earle Birney, "Class in Canadian Literature," *Canadian Literature,* 20 (1964), 77. The best and most detailed description of Birney's early life is in Frank Davey, *Earle Birney* (Toronto, 1971).

2. Birney Collection, Fisher Rare Books Library, University of Toronto. Box 63, "Autobiographical Materials."

3. Earle Birney, *The Cow Jumped Over the Moon* (Toronto, 1972), pp. 4–5.

4. Davey, *Earle Birney,* p. 5.

5. Ibid., p. 6.

6. Desmond Pacey, *Ten Canadian Poets* (Toronto, 1958), pp. 297–98.

7. Davey, *Earle Birney,* pp. 7–9.

8. Ibid., p. 11.

9. Pacey, *Ten Canadian Poets,* p. 300.

10. Birney, *The Cow Jumped Over the Moon,* p. 6.

11. Davey, *Earle Birney,* pp. 20–21.

12. Earle Birney, "Does Canada Owe Her Authors a Living?" *Mayfair* (Montreal) 27 (Feb. 1953), 36, 73.

13. A. J. M. Smith, *The Book of Canadian Poetry* (Toronto, 1948), pp. 27–28.

14. Davey, *Earle Birney,* p. 44.

15. E. J. Pratt, review of *David and Other Poems, Canadian Poetry Magazine,* (March 1943), pp. 34–35.

16. Birney, *The Cow Jumped Over the Moon,* p. 42. In the event, apparently Ryerson did agree to print a second edition.

17. Birney, "The Canadian Writer Versus the Canadian Education," 110.

18. George Herbert Clarke, review of *Now Is Time, Queens Quarterly* 53 (1946), 266.

19. M. H. Martin, review of *Now Is Time, Canadian Forum* 25 (March 1946), 393.

20. Watson Kirkconnell, review of *Now Is Time, Canadian Poetry Magazine* 9 (March 1946), 36.

21. Davey, *Earle Birney,* p. 21.

22. Roy Daniells, review of *Strait of Anian, Canadian Poetry Magazine* 11 (June 1948), 48.

23. Birney, "Has Poetry a Future in Canada?" *Manitoba Arts Review* 5 (Spring 1946), 15.

24. Daniells, *Canadian Poetry Magazine* 11 (June 1948), 48.

25. Birney, "Turvey and the Critics," *Canadian Literature* 30 (1966), 22.

26. Davey, *Earle Birney,* pp. 28–29.

27. Birney, *The Creative Writer,* (Toronto, 1966), p. 41.

28. D. J. Dooley, "The Satiric Novel in Canada Today," *Queens Quarterly,* 64 (1958), 581–83.

29. Birney, "Turvey and the Critics," 24.

30. Ibid., 24–25.

31. Birney, *The Creative Writer,* p. 44.

32. Birney, "Epilogue" in Bruce Nesbitt, ed., *Earle Birney* (Toronto, 1974), p. 216.

33. Birney, *The Creative Writer,* p. 44.

34. Birney, "Turvey and the Critics," 24.

35. L. A. MacKay, review of *Trial of a City and Other Verse, Northern Review,* 6, vol. 4 (Oct.-Nov. 1953), 44.

36. Alan Crawley, review of the radio presentation of *Trial of a City, Contemporary Verse,* 39 (1952), 25.

37. Desmond Pacey, *Creative Writing in Canada* (Toronto, 1952), p. 138.

38. Desmond Pacey, *Ten Canadian Poets* (Toronto, 1958), p. 326.

39. Roy Daniells, "Lorne Pierce Medal," Royal Society of Canada *Transactions,* 3rd series, 47 (1953), 37–38.

40. Earle Birney, *Down the Long Table* (Toronto, 1955, repr. 1975), p. 69.

41. Earle Birney, "Proletarian Literature: Theory and Practice," *Canadian Forum* 17 (May 1937), 59.

42. Birney, *Down the Long Table,* p. 267.

43. Arnold Edinborough, review of *Down the Long Table* in Bruce Nesbitt, *Earle Birney,* p. 97.

44. Davey, *Earle Birney,* p. 41.

45. Birney Collection, letter to Robert Weaver at CBC, Toronto, 20 March 1951.

46. Dooley, "The Satiric Novel in Canada Today," 585.

47. Earle Birney, "Epilogue" in Bruce Nesbitt, *Earle Birney,* pp. 216–17.

48. Birney Collection, letter to Ethel Wilson, 23 October 1958.

49. Not seven, as Frank Davey suggests in *Earle Birney,* p. 27.

50. Pacey, *Ten Canadian Poets,* pp. 325–26.

51. Earle Birney, "The Writer and the H-Bomb: Why Create?" *Queens Quarterly* 62 (1955), 40.

52. John Sutherland, "The Past Decade," *Northern Review* 4/2 (1951), 44.

53. Earle Birney, "Why, You Can't Teach Creative Writing," *Inland* (Salt Lake City) 3 (Summer 1959) 6. Published under the pseudonym of "H. Quincy Bogholder."

54. Davey, *Earle Birney,* pp. 54–55.

55. Birney, "The Writer and the H-Bomb," 41.

56. Al Purdy, review of *Near False Creek Mouth, Fiddlehead,* 65 (1965), 75.

57. Birney, "The Writer and the H-Bomb," 37.

58. Ian McCallum, "Experience Nagging to be Worded — The Art of Earle Birney," *Sheaf,* University of Saskatchewan, (Saskatoon) (27 June 1967), p. 18.

59. A. J. M. Smith, *Book of Canadian Poetry,* p. 30.

60. Northrop Frye, "Canada and Its Poetry," *Canadian Forum* 23 (1943), 208.

61. Earle Birney, *Selected Poems, 1940–1966* (Toronto, 1966), p. ix.

62. Theodore Holmes, review of *Selected Poems, Dalhousie Review,* 47 (Autumn 1967), 265.

63. A. J. M. Smith, "A Unified Personality: Birney's Poems," *Canadian Literature,* 30 (1966), 11–12.

64. George Woodcock, "Turning New Leaves," *Canadian Forum,* 46 (1966), 115.

65. Birney Collection, letter to Earle Birney from Peter Dwyer, Associate Director of the Canada Council, 16 October 1968.

66. Northrop Frye, review of *David and Other Poems, Canadian Forum,* 22 (December 1942), 279.

67. Smith, *Book of Canadian Poetry,* p. 32.

68. Pacey, *Ten Canadian Poets,* pp. 294–95.

Chapter Two

1. Peter C. Noel-Bentley, "Collected Birney," *Contemporary Verse II,* 2, no. 1 (January 1976), 28.

2. Desmond Pacey, *Ten Canadian Poets,* p. 298.

3. Birney, "Epilogue," p. 210.

4. Birney, *Down the Long Table,* p. 63.

5. Ibid., p. 110.

6. Arnold Edinborough, review of *Turvey, Queens Quarterly* 56 (Winter 1949–50), 609.

7. Birney, *Turvey,* p. 222.

8. Ibid., p. 229.

9. F. R. Scott, "How Canada Entered the War," *Canadian Forum* 19 (Feb. 1940), 344–46.

Chapter Three

1. Pacey, *Creative Writing in Canada,* p. 141.
2. Birney, *The Creative Writer,* p. 6.
3. Milton Wilson, "Poet without a Muse," *Canadian Literature* 30 (1966), 19.
4. Much of this interpretation of the poem is derived from Milton Wilson, "Poet without a Muse," 18-19.
5. Later republished as "These With Wind."
6. Birney, *The Cow Jumped Over the Moon,* pp. 86-87.
7. Paul West, "Earle Birney and the Compound Ghost," 9.
8. Earle Birney, "Against the Spell of Death," *Prairie Schooner* 37 (1963-64), 329-30.
9. Birney, *The Creative Writer,* p. 2.
10. George Woodcock, "Turning New Leaves," *Canadian Forum* 46 (1966), 116.
11. Dorothy Livesay, "This Canadian Poetry," *Canadian Forum* 24 (1944), 21.
12. Anonymous, review of *Near False Creek Mouth, Canadian Poetry Magazine* 28 (Feb. 1965), 38-39.
13. Birney, *The Cow Jumped Over the Moon,* pp. 7-8.

Chapter Four

1. Paul West, "Earle Birney and the Compound Ghost," *Canadian Literature* 13 (1962), 5-6.
2. Al Purdy, "The Man Who Killed David," *Weekend Magazine,* no. 50 (14 Dec. 1974), 16-17.
3. Birney, *Turvey,* p. 48.
4. Purdy, "The Man Who Killed David," 17.
5. Milton Wilson, "Poet without a Muse," 19.
6. Davey, *Earle Birney,* pp. 106-107.
7. A. J. M. Smith, "A Unified Personality," 11.
8. Birney, "Epilogue" in Bruce Nesbitt, ed., *Earle Birney,* p. 211.
9. Davey, *Earle Birney,* p. 107.
10. Milton Wilson, review of *Ice Cod Bell or Stone, University of Toronto Quarterly* 32 (April 1963), 368.

Chapter Five

1. Birney Collection, Box 63, "Autobiographical Materials."
2. Birney Collection, letter to the Director of the Marine Biological Station at Friday Harbor, Washington, 17 July 1952.
3. Birney, *The Cow Jumped Over the Moon,* p. 16.

4. W. H. New, "Prisoner of Dreams: The Poetry of Earle Birney," *Canadian Forum* 52 (Sept. 1972), 29.

5. Northrop Frye, "Canada and Its Poetry" (review of A. J. M. Smith's *Book of Canadian Poetry*), *Canadian Forum* 23 (1943), 209.

6. Ibid., 210.

7. Birney, *The Cow Jumped Over the Moon,* p. 7.

8. Margaret Atwood, *Survival: A Thematic Guide to Canadian Literature* (Toronto, 1972), pp. 57–58.

9. Ibid., p. 60.

10. Howard Sergeant, "Poetry of the Commonwealth," *English* 15 (Autumn 1963), 209.

11. Northrop Frye, "Poetry," *University of Toronto Quarterly* 22 (April 1953), 275.

12. Earle Birney, "Random Remarks on a Random World," *Western Humanities Review* 15 (1961), 7.

13. Birney Collection, Box 63, "Autobiographical Materials."

14. Birney, *Down the Long Table,* p. 285.

15. John Sutherland, "Earle Birney's 'David,' " *First Statement* 1/9 (nd), 7.

16. Atwood, *Survival,* p. 63.

Chapter Six

1. See for example Birney's satirical article published under the pseudonym "H. Quincy Bogholder," "Why, You Can't Teach Creative Writing," 3–10.

2. Birney, *The Creative Writer,* p. 13.

3. Pacey, *Ten Canadian Poets,* p. 299.

4. Davey, *Earle Birney,* p. 16.

5. Birney, *The Creative Writer,* pp. 35–36.

6. Birney, "Turvey and the Critics," *Canadian Literature* 30 (1966), 22.

7. Birney, *The Creative Writer,* p. 39. Similar adaptations were made of "Conrad Kain" and "Wind Chimes in a Temple Ruin."

8. Woodcock, "Turning New Leaves," 115.

9. Purdy, "The Man Who Killed David," 17.

10. Birney, *The Cow Jumped Over the Moon,* p. 85.

11. Ibid., p. 21.

12. Peter Noel-Bentley, "Collected Birney," *Contemporary Verse II,* 2, no. 1 (January 1976), 27.

13. This point is fully discussed in Richard Robillard, *Earle Birney* (Toronto, 1971).

14. Birney Collection, letter to Lois Wilson, 24 January 1956.

15. Edinborough, review of *Turvey,* 608.

16. Davey, *Earle Birney,* p. 19.

17. West, "Earle Birney and the Compound Ghost," 8.

18. Earle Birney, ed., *Twentieth Century Canadian Poetry,* (Toronto, 1953), p. xiv.

19. Frye, "Letters in Canada: Poetry 1952–1960," p. 102.

20. Birney, *The Creative Writer,* p. 15.

21. Ralph Hicklin, "Earle Birney and the Poetry of the Beats and the Black Mountains," *Toronto Globe and Mail* (23 April 1966).

22. For a full discussion of the Black Mountain movement see Frank Davey, "Black Day on Black Mountain," *Tamarack Review* 36 (Spring 1965), 62–71.

23. Birney, *The Creative Writer,* p. 75.

24. Ibid., p. 73.

25. Frank Davey, *Earle Birney,* pp. 62–63.

26. bp Nichol, "an introduction," in Earle Birney, *Pnomes Jukollages & other Stunzas,* grOnk, series 4, no. 3 (Toronto, 1969).

27. M. L. Rosenthal, *The New Poets: American and British Poetry Since World War II* (New York, 1967), pp. 146–47.

28. Ralph Hicklin, "Earle Birney and the Poetry of the Beats and the Black Mountains," *Toronto Globe and Mail* (23 April 1966).

29. Birney, *The Creative Writer,* p. 81.

30. Ibid., p. 77.

31. Earle Birney, "Canadian Publishing: Answers to a Questionnaire," *Canadian Literature* 33 (Summer 1967), 12.

32. A. J. M. Smith, "A Unified Personality," 12–13.

33. Birney, *The Cow Jumped Over the Moon,* pp. 15–16.

34. Roy Daniells, "Earle Birney et Robert Finch," *Gants du Ciel* 11 (1946), 85.

35. Roy Daniells, review of *Strait of Anian, Canadian Poetry Magazine* 11 (June 1948), 48.

36. E. J. Pratt, review of *David and Other Poems; Canadian Poetry Magazine* (March 1943), 35.

37. Pacey, *Ten Canadian Poets,* p. 305.

38. Milton Wilson, review of *Near False Creek Mouth,* 350.

39. Pacey, *Ten Canadian Poets,* p. 312.

40. Birney, "War and the English Intellectuals," 110.

41. Pacey, *Ten Canadian Poets,* p. 309.

42. John Robert Colombo, "Poetic Ambassador," *Canadian Literature,* 24 (Spring 1965), 55.

Chapter Seven

1. Smith, *Book of Canadian Poetry,* pp. 28–29.

2. Birney, *The Cow Jumped Over the Moon,* p. 96.

3. Margaret Atwood, *Survival: A Thematic Guide to Canadian Literature* (Toronto, 1972), pp. 95–96.

4. E. K. Brown, review of *Now Is Time, University of Toronto Quarterly,* 15 (1946), 273.

5. Theodore Holmes, review of *Selected Poems, 1940–1966, Dalhousie Review,* 47 (Autumn 1967), 262.

6. Birney, *The Creative Writer,* p. 6.

7. Birney, "E. J. Pratt & His Critics," *Masks of Poetry: Canadian Critics on Canadian Verse,* ed. A. J. M. Smith (Toronto, 1962), p. 93.

8. For a detailed description of Birney's political development see Davey, *Earle Birney,* pp. 1–19.

9. Milton Wilson, "Letters in Canada: Poetry, 1964," *University of Toronto Quarterly* 34 (1965), 350.

10. Davey, *Birney,* p. 98.

11. Birney, *Down the Long Table,* p. 298.

12. Cf. "The Writer and the H-Bomb: Why Create?" *Queen's Quarterly* 62 (1955), 37–44.

13. Birney, "North American Drama Today: A Popular Art?" *Transactions of the Royal Society of Canada,* 3rd series, 51 (section 2) (1957), 41–42.

14. Birney, "The Modern Face of Hubris," p. 59.

15. Birney, *The Cow Jumped Over the Moon,* pp. 90–91.

16. Purdy, "The Man Who Killed David," 17.

17. Frye, "Letters in Canada: Poetry 1952–1960," p. 101.

Selected Bibliography

PRIMARY SOURCES

1. Manuscripts and Documents

Birney Collection. Fisher Rare Books Library. University of Toronto. Correspondence, drafts of poems and stories, scrap-books, personal papers reaching back almost to Birney's birth.

2. Poetry

The Collected Poems of Earle Birney. Toronto: McClelland and Stewart, 1975.

David and Other Poems. Toronto: Ryerson, 1942.

Ice Cod Bell or Stone: a Collection of New Poems. Toronto: McClelland and Stewart, 1962.

Memory no Servant. Trumansburg, N.Y.: New Books, 1968.

Near False Creek Mouth: New Poems. Toronto: McClelland and Stewart, 1964.

Now is Time. Toronto: Ryerson, 1945.

Pnomes Jukollages & other Stunzas. grOnk, series 4, no. 3. Toronto: Ganglia Press, 1969.

The Poems of Earle Birney; a New Canadian Library Selection with an Introduction by the Author. Toronto: McClelland and Stewart, 1969.

rag & bone shop. Toronto: McClelland and Stewart, 1971.

The Rugging and the Moving Times: Poems New and Uncollected. Coatsworth, Ont.: Black Moss Press, 1976.

Selected Poems: 1940–1966. Toronto: McClelland and Stewart, 1966.

The Strait of Anian: Selected Poems. Toronto: Ryerson, 1948.

Trial of a City and Other Verse. Toronto: Ryerson, 1953.

what's so big about GREEN? Toronto: McClelland and Stewart, 1973.

3. Fiction

Down the Long Table. Toronto: McClelland, 1955.

Turvey; a Military Picaresque. Toronto: McClelland, 1949.

4. Anthology

Birney, Earle, ed. *Twentieth Century Canadian Poetry; an Anthology with Introduction and Notes.* Toronto: Ryerson, 1953.

172

5. Criticism

"Against the Spell of Death." *Prairie Schooner* 37 (1963–64), 328–33. A discussion of the poetry of Malcolm Lowry.

"Canadian Publishing: Answers to a Questionnaire." *Canadian Literature* 33 (Summer 1967), 5–15.

"The Canadian Writer Versus the Canadian Education." *Evidence* 10 (1967), 97–113.

"Class in Canadian Literature." *Canadian Literature* 20 (1964), 77–78. Discussion of Birney's own proletarian origins.

The Cow Jumped Over the Moon: the Writing and Reading of Poetry. Toronto: Holt, Rinehart and Winston, 1972.

The Creative Writer. Toronto: Canadian Broadcasting Corporation Publications, 1966. Text of a series of radio broadcasts.

"Does Canada Owe Her Authors a Living?" *Mayfair* (Montreal) 27 (Feb. 1953), 36, 73–75.

"E. J. Pratt and His Critics" in *Masks of Poetry: Canadian Critics on Canadian Verse.* Ed. A. J. M. Smith. Toronto: 1962, pp. 72–95.

"Epilogue" in *Earle Birney.* Ed. Bruce Nesbitt. Toronto: McGraw-Hill Ryerson, pp. 206–18. Birney's rejoinders to the various critics whom Nesbitt has included in his book.

"The Many Faces of Vancouver." *Century* (13 Feb. 1967), 44–46.

"The Modern Face of Hubris" in *Hubris, Man and Education.* Ed. J. Allan Ross. Bellingham: Union Printing Co., 1959, pp. 46–60.

"New Verse." *Canadian Forum* 20 (Oct. 1940), 221.

"North American Drama Today: a Popular Art?" *Transactions of the Royal Society of Canada,* 3rd series, 51 (section 2, 1957), 31–42.

"Proletarian Literature: Theory and Practice." *Canadian Forum* 17 (May 1937), 58–60.

"Random Remarks on a Random World." *Western Humanities Review* 15 (1961), 3–10.

"Turvey and the Critics." *Canadian Literature* 30 (1966), 22.

"War and the English Intellectuals." *Canadian Forum* 21 (1941), 110–14.

"Why, You Can't Teach Creative Writing." *Inland* (Salt Lake City) 3 (Summer 1959), 3–10. Published under pseudonym of "H. Quincy Bogholder, Ph.D., F.R.S.B.K."

"The Writer and the H-Bomb: Why Create?" *Queen's Quarterly* 62 (1955), 37–44.

SECONDARY SOURCES

ALLEN, DONALD M. *The New American Poetry.* New York: Grove, 1960. A discussion of the Black Mountain movement.

ATWOOD, MARGARET. *Survival: a Thematic Guide to Canadian Literature.* Toronto: Anansi, 1972. An examination of some of the dominant motifs in Canadian literature.

COLOMBO, JOHN ROBERT. "Poetic Ambassador." *Canadian Literature* 24 (Spring 1965), 55–59. Comments upon Birney's poetry in relationship to his travels.

DANIELLS, ROY. "Earle Birney et Robert Finch." *Gants du Ciel* 11 (1946), 83–96. One of the early acknowledgments of Birney's importance in the field of poetry.

———. "Lorne Pierce Medal." Royal Society of Canada, *Proceedings and Transactions,* 3rd series, 47 (1953), 37–38. Text of speech made on the occasion of Birney being awarded the Lorne Pierce Medal.

DAVEY, FRANK. "Black Days on Black Mountain." *Tamarack Review* 36 (Spring 1965), 62–71. An attempt to review the Black Mountain movement and especially its impact on poetry.

———. *Earle Birney.* Toronto: Copp-Clark, 1971. A useful short summary of Birney's life and work.

DOOLEY, D. J. "The Satiric Novel in Canada Today." *Queen's Quarterly* 64 (1958), 576–90. Includes discussion of both *Turvey* and *Down the Long Table.*

DUDEK, LOUIS. "Lunchtime Reflections on Frank Davey's Defence of the Black Mountain Fort." *Tamarack Review* 36 (Summer 65), 58–63. Dudek, as poet, records some differing opinions of the Black Mountain movement.

FRYE, NORTHROP. "Canada and its Poetry." *Canadian Forum* 23 (1943), 207–10. A review of the major trends apparent in Canadian poetry in the early 1940s.

———. "Poetry." *University of Toronto Quarterly* 22 (April 1953), 269–80. A discussion of the work of the more important writers, including Birney, to have appeared in recent years.

HICKLIN, RALPH. "Earle Birney and the Poetry of the Beats and the Black Mountains." An attempt to clarify some of the principal tenets of the Black Mountain school of poetry and its relationship to Birney's work.

LIVESAY, DOROTHY. "This Canadian Poetry." *Canadian Forum* 24 (1944), 20–21. A survey of contemporary trends in Canadian poetry.

MCCALLUM, IAN. "Experience Nagging to be Worded — the Art of Earle Birney." *Sheaf* (University of Saskatchewan, Saskatoon, 27 June 1967), 18–19. Radio interview with Birney, covering wide range of opinion and including the reading of some poems.

MACCULLOCH, CLAIRE. "Earle Birney on the Spit." *Books in Canada* 3 (April 1975), 3–4. Review of *Collected Poems.*

NESBITT, BRUCE, ed. *Earle Birney.* Toronto: McGraw-Hill Ryerson, 1974. A collection of representative critical essays on Birney.

NEW, W. H. "Prisoner of Dreams: the Poetry of Earle Birney." *Canadian Forum* 52 (Sep. 1972), 29–32. An examination of the effect of history and tradition upon Birney's work and thought.

NOEL-BENTLEY, PETER C. "Collected Birney." *Contemporary Verse II* 2, no. 1 (January 1976), 27–29. Review of *Collected Poems*.

————, and EARLE BIRNEY. "Earle Birney: a Bibliography in Progress, 1923–1969." *West Coast Review*, V, 2 (Oct. 1970), 45–53. An indispensable tool for any research on Birney's life and work. Includes dates and places of first publication of poems and short stories.

PACEY, DESMOND. *Creative Writing in Canada*. Toronto: Ryerson, 1952. An examination of major trends among contemporary Canadian writers.

————. "Earle Birney," in *Ten Canadian Poets*. Toronto: Ryerson, 1958, pp. 293–326. A chapter devoted to Birney's life and work.

PURDY, AL. "The Man Who Killed David." *Weekend Magazine* 24, no. 50 (14 Dec. 1974), 16–17.

ROBILLARD, RICHARD. *Earle Birney*. Toronto: McClelland and Stewart, 1971. Very useful for its discussion of Birney's prosody.

ROSENTHAL, M. L. *The New Poets: American and British Poetry Since World War II*. One section is devoted to a discussion of the Black Mountain poets; also includes comments upon the writing of concrete poetry.

SCOTT, F. R. "How Canada Entered the War." *Canadian Forum* 19 (February 1940), 344–46. An enlightening article on the motives of the Canadian government in 1939.

SERGEANT, HOWARD. "Poetry of the Commonwealth." *English* (England) 15 (Autumn 1963), 209. Discusses the effect of strange landscapes and climates upon poets of Anglo-Saxon origin.

SMITH, A. J. M., ed. *The Book of Canadian Poetry. A Critical and Historical Anthology*. With an Introduction and Notes, rev. and enl. Toronto: Gage, 1948. A standard anthology from pre-Confederation times up to the date of publication. Includes very useful prefatory essays on each poet.

————. "A Unified Personality: Birney's Poems." *Canadian Literature* 30 (1966), 4–13. A discussion of *Selected Poems* in light of Birney's life and his development as a poet.

SUTHERLAND, JOHN. "The Past Decade." *Northern Review* 4/2 (1951), 44. A review of the effect of the political events of the 1940s upon Canada's poets and their work.

WARR, BERTRAM. *Acknowledgment to Life*. Foreword by Earle Birney. Toronto: Ryerson, 1970. Poems.

WELLS, HENRY WILLIS. *Where Poetry Stands Now*. Toronto: Ryerson, 1948. Discussion of the work of six Canadian poets, including Birney.

WEST, PAUL. "Earle Birney and the Compound Ghost." *Canadian Literature* 13 (1962), 5–14. Review of *Ice Cod Bell or Stone*.

WILSON, MILTON. "Letters in Canada: Poetry, 1964." *University of Toronto Quarterly* 34 (1965), 349–51. Includes a review of *Near False Creek Mouth*.

_____. "Poet Without a Muse." *Canadian Literature* 30 (1966), 14–20.
Uses the publication of *Selected Poems* as an occasion to discuss the
influences, or lack of influences, upon Birney's poetic development.

Index

Birney, Earle (1904–), awarded Canada Council medal, 44; and the Beat poets, 123, 150; beginning of poetic career, 16; and censorship, 29; Chaucer, studies on, 14, 32, effect of, 53, 121, 153; childhood, 100, 111; and the Cold War, 27, 29, 32, 150; concern for ecosystem, 54, 58-59, 150-52; concrete poetry, 36, 45, 135-37; development of poetic style, 24; early education, 13, 14; early poetic output, 15; as editor of *Canadian Forum*, 16, 31; editor of *Ubyssey*, 14; Eliot and Auden, reaction against, 21, 141; and explorers, 23, 61, 146; fantasies of flying, 70; Great Depression, the, influence on, 15, 29, 72, 153; influenced by Auden, Spender and Day Lewis, 15, 113; and McCarthyism, 27, 30, 32; on marriage, 47-48, 76-80; 1960's, influence upon, 41, 81; on nuclear warfare, 32, 33, 35, 156; opinion of Canada, 23, 29, 43, 46, 71-72, 98-99, 119, 149, 161-62; parents' characters, 13, 14, 153; parents' origins, 13; political views, 31, 33, 34; and racism, 29, 57, 58; and religion, 50, 54-55, 86, 94, 158-59; as reviser, 122-23; similarities with Swift, 28, 55, 97, 152; as soldier, 16, 19; as sun worshipper, 111-14; and Trotskyism, 15; Turvey, resemblance to, 25, 61; university education, 14-16; as university teacher, 15, 16, 22, 39-41; and Vancouver, 27, 51; on Viet Nam war, 49, 151, 161; as working man, 14, 15, 147; as world traveller, 22, 34-36, 37-38, 44, 51, 98, 141; World War II, influence upon, 16, 18, 19, 21, 23-24, 29, 78, 153-56; youth, 14

WORKS–DRAMA:

Damnation of Vancouver, The (*Trial of a City*), 42-43, 69, 71, 100, 117, 120, 124, 126-27, 133, 138, 148, 157, 163

WORKS–NOVELS:

Down the Long Table, 30-32, 59-60, 74, 76, 110, 113, 131, 144, 145, 157-58

Turvey, 24-26, 32; unexpurgated version, 51, 60-67, 83, 91, 131, 145

WORKS–POETRY:

Collected Poems, 51

David and Other Poems, 16, 17-19, 118

Ice Cod Bell or Stone, 32, 34-36

Near False Creek Mouth, 36-39, 81

Now is Time, 20, 21-22, 24, 149, 155

pnomes, jukollages and other stunzas, 45

Poems of Earle Birney, The, 44

rag & bone shop, 34, 44, 45-48

Rugging and the Moving Times, The, 51

Selected Poems, 41-44

Strait of Anian, 22-24, 155

Trial of a City and Other Verse, 26-29, 55

what's so big about GREEN?, 48-51

WORKS–INDIVIDUAL POEMS:

"Adagio", 79

"Alaska Passage", 45, 137

"Aluroid", 74, 89-90, 93, 118

"And the Earth Grow Young Again", 149

"Anglosaxon street", 16, 37, 57, 110, 122, 123, 126, 149

"Appeal to a lady with a diaper", 36, 45, 120, 132, 136

"ARRIVALS—Wolfville", 104, 142, 147

"Atlantic door", 22, 43, 103, 105, 108, 109, 110, 111, 146
"Atoll", 119
"Ballad of Kootenay Brown", 85, 138, 139
"Ballad of Mr. Chubb", 42, 73, 77, 120
"Bangkok boy", 82, 85, 113, 125-26
"Bear on the Delhi Road, The", 21, 85, 87-88, 109, 128
"Billboards build freedom of choice", 54
"Biography", 43, 81, 82, 115
"Buenos Aires: 1962", 160
"Buildings", 136
"Bushed", 43, 89-90, 103, 104, 106, 107, 108, 117
"Cadet hospital", 74
"Campus theatre steps", 45, 144
"Canada: case history: 1945", 24
"Canada: case history: 1973", 161-62
"Candidate's prayer before master's oral", 40
"Can. Lit.", 98
"Captain Cook", 109, 132
"Caracas", 159
"Caribbean kingdoms", 38, 101, 130-31
"Cartagena de Indias, 1962", 38-39, 159
"Charité espérance et foi", 71, 148
"Christmas comes. . .", 29, 98
"Climbers", 43, 105, 120, 129, 142
"Conducted ritual: San Juan de Ulúa", 58
"Conrad Kain", 104, 124, 138-39, 140, 144-46, 156
"Cucurachas in paradise", 49, 55, 70, 71, 106, 138, 150
" Curaçao", 68
"David", 16, 18, 21, 22, 39, 43, 73, 81, 83, 91, 103, 104, 105, 107, 108, 113, 115, 118, 120, 124-25, 128, 129, 132, 138, 139, 142, 144-46
"Daybreak on Lake Opal: High Rockies", 49, 111, 112, 118
"D-Day", 105
"Death of a war", 20
"Dusk on English Bay", 16, 24, 109, 128-29, 131, 154

"Ebb begins from dream, The", 57, 78-79, 110, 147-48
"El Greco: Espolio", 35, 86-87, 158
"Ellesmereland I", 35, 55, 119
"Epidaurus", 135
"ESTHER", 135
"First tree for frost", 68, 74, 109
"Flying fish" ("Poem"), 85, 101, 110, 118, 128-29
"For maister Geffrey", 45, 46
"For Steve", 24, 73, 116, 128, 153-54, 156
"Found Paean to Vancouver by Rudyard Kipling, 1890", 162
"Found Swahili serenade/a jukollage", 79, 137
"Four feet between", 21, 47, 138, 143, 149
"Francisco Tresguerras", 127
"From the hazel bough", 43, 73, 76-77, 81, 83
"Giovanni Caboto/John Cabot", 71
"God", 50
"Gray woods exploding, The", 21, 79, 83, 113, 117, 138, 139, 140, 144
"Grey-Rocks", 119
"Gulf of Georgia", 43-44, 109
"Haiku for a young waitress", 43, 82
"Halifax", 115-16
"Hands", 17-18, 108, 112, 118, 149, 154
"Holiday in the foothills", 67
"Honolulu", 126
"Hot Springs", 56
"I accuse us", 49, 161
"If you were here", 83
"I think you are a whole city", 48, 80
"Images in place of logging", 107, 150
"In Purdy's Ameliasburg", 106, 118
"In this verandah", 94, 116
"Introvert", 117, 130
"Invasion spring", 75, 105
"Joe Harris", 13, 34, 83, 116; adaptations of, 122, 144-46; 147, 149, 153-54, 156
"Kootenay still-life", 101
"Lament", 77

"Late afternoon in Manzanillo", 56, 93

"Leaving the park", 104-105, 114-15

"Letter to a conceivable great-grand-son", 42

"Letter to a Cuzco Priest", 134-35, 160

"Like an eddy", 45, 48

"Lines for a peace", 20

"Looking from Oregon", 161

"Machu Picchu", 94-95

"Mammorial stunzas for Aimee Simple McFarcin", 54-55, 133

"Mammoth corridors", 47, 55, 107, 109, 120, 148, 152

"Man is a snow", 24, 114, 155

"Man on a tractor", 115, 147, 149, 156

"Mappemounde", 78, 109, 123-24

"Maritime faces", 105, 111

"Marriage, The", 77-78

"Meeting of strangers", 68-69

"Memory no servant", 134

"Men's sportswear dept.", 49

"Miracle is the stream, The", 84

"Monody of a century", 78, 154

"Moon down Elphinstone", 51, 138, 139, 156

"Most of a dialogue in Cuzco", 57, 160

"Museum of man", 46, 47, 68

"Nayarít", 136

"New Brunswick", 22

"1984 minus 17 & counting at u of waterloo ont", 40

"North of Superior", 90, 91-92, 108, 115, 151

"North Star west", 87, 108, 110, 118

"November walk near False Creek mouth", 33-34, 37, 88-89, 97, 109, 148

"October in Utah", 15, 113

"Oil refinery", 91, 152

"Oldster", 101, 127

"Omnibus", 84

"Once high upon a hill", 46-47

"On a diary", 21, 77, 113-14, 117

"On her twenty-sixth birthday", 84, 140

"On the beach", 68, 83

"...or a wind", 114, 155

"O what can i do", 78

"Pachucan miners", 35, 91, 95, 123, 130

"Pacific door", 22, 23, 43, 146-47

"Page of Gaspé", 118, 150

"Perth, Australia, I love you", 101-102

"Plaza de la Inquisición", 55

"Poem" *see* "Flying fish"

"Pnome", 46, 49

"Prairie counterpoint", 22, 102, 119, 128-29

"Professor of Middle English confronts monster", 70

"Québec May", 22, 24, 43, 126

"Reading the diary" *see* "On a diary"

"Remarks decoded from outer space", 20, 23, 42, 55, 122

"Reverse on the Coast Range", 106, 107

"Road to Nijmegen", 21, 73, 75, 113, 122, 150

"St. Valentine is past", 73, 75-76, 81, 82

"Sestina for the Ladies of Tehuántepec", 160

"Shapers: Vancouver, The", 50, 148

"She is", 117, 123

"Sinalóa", 149, 151

"Six-sided square: Actopan", 69, 90-91, 149

"Sixth grade biology quiz", 35, 55, 119, 127-28

"Slug in woods", 101, 106, 107, 109, 110, 118, 131

"Small port in the outer Fijis", 93, 149, 152

"Song for sunsets", 47, 111-12

"State of Sonora", 130

"Still", 78, 110, 136-37

"Sunday nightfall in Winnipeg", 103, 120

"Sunrise on Lake Opal", 50

"Takkakaw falls", 43, 89-90, 92, 107, 124, 146

"Tavern by the Hellespont", 80, 96

"Tea at my Shetland aunt's", 45, 70, 71

"There are delicacies", 48, 136
"This page my pigeon", 73, 75, 76
"To a Hamilton (Ont.) lady thinking to travel", 57-58, 149
"Toronto march", 106
"Toronto Board of Trade goes abroad", 94, 103
"To Swindon from London by Britrail aloud/Bagatelle", 125
"Transcontinental", 107, 119
"Transistor", 36-37, 96, 127-28
"Turbonave magnolia", 144
"21st century belongs to the moon, The", 50, 86
"Twenty-third flight", 68, 82, 120
"Ulysses", 155
"Underkill", 49, 162
"Up her can nada", 135, 137
"Vancouver lights", 16, 18-19, 94, 109, 153
"VE-Night", 23
"Vitus Bering", 132
"Wake Island", 110, 111, 132
"Walk in Kyoto, A", 82, 143-44
"War winters", 112, 124, 154
"Way to the west", 44, 134-35, 150, 151
"What's so big about GREEN?", 49, 107-108, 118, 148
"Wind-chimes in a temple ruin", 77
"Window seat", 46, 47
"Winter Saturday", 103, 109, 119
"Within these caverned days", 73
"World conference", 20, 21, 24
"Young veterans", 20
WORKS – SHORT STORIES:
"Enigma in Ebony", 126
"Mickey was a Swell Guy", 74, 144
"The Reverend Eastham Discovers Life", 115

Bissett, Bill, 135, 136
Black Mountain poets, the, 41, 123, 133-34, 136
Bolívar, Simon, 159-60

Dos Passos, John, influence on Birney, 31
Dudek, Louis, 17

Edgar, Pelham, 15, 16

Joyce, James, influence on Birney, 28, 31, 45, 69, 121, 133

Knister, Raymond, 17

Lampman, Archibald, 17
Livesay, Dorothy, 17
Lopez, Luis, 38, 160
Lowry, Malcolm, poetry edited by Birney, 44; Birney on, 79, 103

Marriott, Anne, 17
Montreal Group, the, 29

Neruda, Pablo, 160
nichol, bp, 45, 135, 136

Pratt, E.J., 29, 98, 108, 138, 148, 152

Sandburg, Carl, 152
Sedgewick, Garnett, 14
Souster, Raymond, 17
Suknaski, Andy, 45

Trotsky, Leon, Literature and Revolution, 15

Warr, Bertram, 44